UNWED & UNBOTHERED

UNWED & UNBOTHERED

The Defiant Lives of Single Women
Throughout History

Emma Duval

Andrews McMeel
PUBLISHING®

Andrews McMeel Publishing
a division of Andrews McMeel Universal
1130 Walnut Street, Kansas City, Missouri 64106

www.andrewsmcmeel.com

25 26 27 28 29 TE2 10 9 8 7 6 5 4 3 2 1

ISBN: 979-8-8816-0003-7

Library of Congress Control Number: 2025934709

Editor: Katie Gould
Art Director/Designer: Tiffany Meairs
Production Editor: Brianna Westervelt
Production Manager: Tamara Haus

MIX
Paper | Supporting
responsible forestry
FSC www.fsc.org **FSC® C016973**

Andrews McMeel Publishing is committed to the responsible use of natural resources
and is dedicated to understanding, measuring, and reducing the impact of our products on
the natural world. By choosing this product, you are supporting responsible management of
the world's forests. The FSC® label means that the materials used for this product come from
well-managed FSC®-certified forests, recycled materials, and other controlled sources.

ATTENTION: SCHOOLS AND BUSINESSES
Andrews McMeel books are available at quantity discounts with bulk purchase
for educational, business, or sales promotional use. For information, please email
the Andrews McMeel Publishing Special Sales Department:
sales@andrewsmcmeel.com.

CONTENTS

PREFACE

"You can be anything, but you must be a wife and mother too."

Growing up, I remember feeling like I could do anything I set my mind to . . . except be single for too long. "You can be anything, but you must be a wife and mother too" seemed to be society's motto. But what if I didn't want to get married and have children? My reluctance wasn't about love itself; I have always been a hopeless romantic. Rather, it came from a certain apprehension about what being a wife would mean, based on my own observations of the married women around me. Watching my female relatives exert themselves for their families, husbands, and children—all while putting their own needs last—felt like a stifling and suffocating future.

As a teenager, I was adamant that I did not want to marry, ever! The reactions in my family varied from dismissive laughter ("You'll change your mind when you get older!") to indignation ("How can you say such a thing?") and worry ("But you'll be so lonely and miserable"). To find comfort, I turned to coming-of-age novels, especially those with female heroines. I became captivated by the ever-outspoken Jo March, the subtly defiant Elizabeth Bennet, and the determined Jane Eyre. Sure, their stories all ended with marriage, but these characters were not meekly submitting to societal expectations; they followed their own hearts, principles, and desires. Their tenacity in asserting agency over their own lives was inspiring to me.

Once I grew older, I realized that the idea of a woman remaining single, especially by choice, was seen by many as a threat to the order of things. The pressure to conform was especially strong coming from religion (in my case, Catholicism) and the media. But what was it about women not being attached to a husband and children that was so menacing? Why, everywhere I looked, was there constant messaging that my fulfillment as a woman would be found primarily through marriage?

I struggled with trying to fit those ideals while also wanting to resist them. Ultimately, I was associating marriage with a rigid set of norms, but I realized that even if I married, I didn't have to conform to the traditional standards. I didn't have to replicate certain dynamics if I didn't want to. As of now, I have been happily married to my husband for almost a decade. We have created our own vision of marriage, one that includes the decision to pursue a childfree life. Not having children has allowed me to be released from the inescapable and unattainable expectations placed on mothers. It hasn't been a complete liberation from gender norms and societal expectations, but it has certainly alleviated that pressure.

Understanding the Roots of the Modern-Day Single Woman

Growing up, there were a few single women I personally knew who really made an impression on me: there was my mom's friend who was always traveling abroad to produce documentaries; a neighbor who had been part of the hippie lifestyle in the 1960s and talked fondly about living in a communal house with multiple friends; and the third, who worked in arts and culture and attended concerts, operas, and ballets for work. In comparison to the life of married women I knew, being single seemed so much more desirable.

As I worked to untangle my vision of womanhood from marriage and motherhood, I knew I wanted to look at history to understand how the modern-day single woman came to be. What insights could I get from these historical roots? Some have blamed modern feminism for promoting financial independence, individuality, and sexual freedom, which are seen as "destroying" the institutions of marriage and the family. Was that true, or did those values predate the second wave of feminism in the 1960s? Would I find demographic, economic, or cultural patterns that could explain the presence of single women in certain times or countries? Did any of these women express critical views about the institution of marriage, or was their perception of marriage idealized? My goal was to see how far back I could go and how many stories I could find.

To do so, I started by defining the scope and scale of my project: I chose to specifically focus on women who never married at all. The reason for that choice, which excludes widows and divorced women, is because as women who at one time were married, their social status and legal rights were different from those of never-married women. I also decided not to include women who were forced into slavery or prostitution because while deserving of documentation and respect, they lacked agency and autonomy over their own marital status and reproductive choices. As much as possible, I wanted to center my research around free choice. It's also important to note that while this book has been informed by my own personal European perspective, I have aimed to present a global and intersectional overview by showcasing a diversity of ethnicities, cultures, and religions.

The results? An abundance of stories! In my research, single women emerged throughout the centuries as passionate artists, fierce activists, disciplined scientists, prolific writers, altruistic social reformers, and generous philanthropists.

I also found that women's choice to (not) marry was influenced to various degrees by economic and demographic factors, employment opportunities, legal rights, and religious affiliation. Remaining single, in itself, wasn't always a viable option for women. When socially accepted alternatives to marriage were nonexistent, women faced the risk of becoming destitute or outcasts. In certain religions (such as Christianity, Buddhism, Jainism, and Daoism), women were able to pursue an unmarried and celibate path through religious orders, but in most cultures, lifelong singleness was thoroughly discouraged. Given these limitations, I viewed the fact that I had been able to compile a list of over five hundred single women as an exciting success.

Some Methodology and Thoughts on Researching Women's History

How would I choose which of these hundreds of women to highlight? First, I decided to set specific and objective limitations: I would avoid women who lacked the agency or legal right to make a choice to marry or not. This included enslaved women (because of the oppressive nature of their status) but also lesbians, since many lived with long-term partners in relationships that could not be legally recognized as marriage even if they wanted to. For example, in 1834, the English landowner Anne Lister exchanged rings and marriage vows with her romantic partner, Ann Walker, before attending a religious service at church to consecrate their union. While this was not a legally or religiously recognized ceremony, they considered themselves as married afterward. Lister and Walker were not the only lesbian couple to "marry" symbolically; the American actress Charlotte Cushman also exchanged rings and vows with her lover, the sculptor Emma Stebbins, around 1858. Who knows how many more lesbian couples would have married if same-sex marriage had been legally recognized? Because marriage has—historically—been a heterosexual institution, I decided not to include single women whose same-sex relationships mirrored the behaviors of (heterosexual) married couples.

I therefore focused on single women whose lives could really demonstrate, through their story or their own words, what I wanted to show, which is the rich, fulfilling, exceptional lives they led as well as their thoughts on marriage and singlehood.

After narrowing my list, I needed to find enough information on each woman to write a short biography. This sometimes proved more difficult than I anticipated. Many of these women were mentioned in history books but often not featured prominently. Thankfully, the work of women historians filled the gaps that were left in the general history publications.

Broad context was provided by history books that examined specific time periods or cultures, such as:

- *The Oxford Encyclopedia of Women in World History* (2008), by Bonnie G. Smith
- *The Creation of Feminist Consciousness: From the Middle Ages to Eighteen-Seventy* (1993), by Gerda Lerner
- *Women and Gender in Medieval Europe: An Encyclopedia* (2006), by Margaret Schaus
- *Women and Gender in Islam: Historical Roots of a Modern Debate* (1992), by Leila Ahmed
- *The Inner Quarters: Marriage and the Lives of Chinese Women in the Sung Period* (1993), by Patricia Ebrey

I was also able to refer to books written specifically about single women, including but not limited to:

- *Singlewomen in the European Past, 1250–1800* (1998), by Judith M. Bennett and Amy M. Froide
- *Spinster: Making a Life of One's Own* (2015), by Kate Bolick
- *All the Single Ladies: Unmarried Women and the Rise of an Independent Nation* (2016), by Rebecca Traister
- *Never Married: Singlewomen in Early Modern England* (2005), by Amy M. Froide
- *Liberty, a Better Husband* (1984), by Lee Virginia Chambers-Schiller
- *A History of Celibacy* (1999), by Elizabeth Abbott
- *Bachelor Girl: The Secret History of Single Women in the Twentieth Century* (2002), by Betsy Israel
- *Women Alone: Spinsters in England, 1660–1850* (2001), by Bridget Hill
- *Alone! Alone! Lives of Some Outsider Women* (2004), by Rosemary Dinnage

A key part in my own research was finding full-length biographies of my subjects. More often than not, if they even existed, they were the work of women historians. I couldn't cite all of them here, but they are mentioned in the bibliography at the end. I wouldn't have been able to write this book without the work of the historians, researchers, and writers who helped bring to light the lives of these women.

After gathering the necessary information, I needed to figure out the best way to present it. I thought about selecting fifty profiles and grouping them by category (athletes, writers, scientists) or doing a chronological study, century by century. I chose to do a little bit of both, as you will see in this book. Each chapter presents single women whose lives illustrate a specific theme that has resonated with me, such as the importance of financial independence, the rejection of gender norms, or the desire to pursue a passion.

Before diving into the individual stories of these fascinating women, a brief overview of the ways in which single women have been judged, pressured, and discriminated against is necessary. Why? Because it demonstrates a long-standing prejudice, one that explains why a project that uplifts the lives of single women is relevant to twenty-first-century readers and feminists.

INTRODUCTION

Single Women as Stereotypes: A Brief Historical Overview

Why write about single women? Are their lives that different from the lives of married women? Maybe not as much today, but single women have long been stereotyped as vain, self-absorbed, deficient, unattractive, and generally inferior to the idealized version of womanhood.

This chapter provides a brief overview of the prejudicial ways in which Western society has continuously treated childless, single women. It aims to present information that will emphasize the need for positive portrayals of single women and their lives and legacies.

The Contrasts, printed circa 1898. A *jeune et bonne mère* (a youthful and good mother) compared to a *vieille coquette* (an old flirt), who is depicted as vain (with her chin up and a smirk), unattractive (with her harsh facial features), and childless (as implied by the small dog). Courtesy of Paris Musées.

The Old Maid, 1777. Courtesy of the Library of Congress, Prints and Photographs Division.

"Spinster." This English term originally described women who spun thread and yarn for a living, but in the eighteenth century, the word became a derogatory catchall for unmarried and childless women over the age of 25. This evolution is in part attributed to misogynistic views toward women who were older, earned their own living, and—according to society—hadn't fulfilled their duty to marry and have children. Still in use today, "spinster" evokes an imagery that casts single women as unattractive, lonely, quirky, and unworthy.

Unfortunately, the word isn't alone or unique in being utilized as a way to negatively portray single women. "Old maid" and "thornback," now out-of-date and archaic, were once just as commonly used as "spinster," and in the Middle Ages, "singlewoman" could be a synonym for "prostitute."[1] Society's unending creativity in finding ways to belittle single women through vocabulary is even more evident considering the fact that single men enjoy the benefit of being called "bachelors," a term that doesn't suffer from negative connotations.

English isn't the only language to be prejudiced against single women: unmarried women over the age of 25 have been called "Christmas cake" in Japan—because they are both past their prime after the twenty-fifth—and "leftover women" in China. For centuries in France, women over the age of 25 who were unmarried by the Feast of Saint Catherine (a martyred virgin), on November 25, were nicknamed "Catherinettes." So far, I haven't come across any synonyms, in any language, that apply to unmarried men in their mid-twenties or older.

The print titled *Old Maids at a Cat's Funeral* (1789, below) depicts a procession of older women carrying their cats, in a graveyard next to a church, as they attend the burial of a friend's deceased pet, and *An Old Maid, Treating a Favorite Cat to a Duck and Green Peas* (1792, bottom) shows a very unattractive woman with an enlarged chin, nose, and forehead; a severe underbite; and hairy eyebrows who lets her cat eat from her own plate of food.

Old maids at a cat's funeral: a funeral procession of elderly women with cats in their arms, following the coffin of a dead cat, in a churchyard, 1789. Courtesy of the Wellcome Collection.

An Old Maid, Treating a Favorite Cat to a Duck and Green Peas, 1792.
Courtesy of the Yale Center for British Art, Paul Mellon Collection.

An Old Coquette Outstood Her Market, circa 1815, by Thomas Rowlandson.
Courtesy of the Yale Center for British Art, Paul Mellon Collection.

Alongside the misogynistic use of vocabulary, printed caricatures were another way that stereotypes about single women were distributed and shared. Satirical illustrations of never-married women emerged in the eighteenth century, such as *The Old Maid* (1777, p. xvi), which denotes the same "childless cat lady" trope that still exists today. These portraits represent the usual stereotype associated with single women: the "crazy" cat lady. As we can see, this offensive portrayal isn't new to the twenty-first century; it already existed over two hundred years ago and has been embedded in our cultural background ever since.

Even though drawings are perhaps the most convenient medium to convey stereotypes, literature has also played a part in cultivating the negative perception of female singleness.

The flawed representation of single women in literary works tends to be more subtle and therefore more insidious than in visual arts.

For example, in fiction, particularly in coming-of-age novels aimed at girls and young women, marriage is presented as the rite of passage to adulthood. This is so ingrained in storytelling that even the most fiercely independent heroines marry by the end, such as Anne Shirley from the Anne of Green Gables series, Meg Murry from the Time Quintet series, or Jo March in *Little Women*—an ending that is known to have been imposed by the publisher against the author's own wishes.

The Assembly of Old Maids, 1743, by Thomas Booth. Courtesy of Yale University Library.

An Old Maid, 1808, by Thomas Rowlandson. Courtesy of the MET Museum.

Rare Specimens of Comparative Craniology: An Old Maid's Skull Phrenologised,
circa 1815. Courtesy of the Library of Congress.

Adult single women, on the other hand, have often been portrayed in a bleak manner. In fairy tales and folklore, for instance, witches and other female villains are usually older women who live alone and cause harm to children.

Starting in the nineteenth century, the increase in visibility of single women without children led to more and more public reactions against what was perceived as selfishness and other moral flaws. In 1869, the essayist William Rathbone Greg published a pamphlet titled *Why Are Women Redundant?* in which he admonished the "enormous and increasing number of single women in the nation."[2] He believed that this phenomenon was "indicative of an unwholesome social state" and that by dodging their "natural duties" as wives and mothers, these unmarried and childless women "lead an independent and incomplete existence of their own." Even the women's magazine *Harper's Bazaar* published in 1895 an article titled "Lone Women," which berated "spinsters, who, not having fulfilled the destiny of their sex, created to be the helpmeet of man, are presumed to be depressed by their failure, and consequently joyless, unsatisfied beings."[3]

To fully understand the weight of the discrimination faced by single women, we also need to look at how they were treated in the eyes of the law. In a patriarchal society that valued women as wives and mothers, single women (widowed, divorced, or never married) found themselves on the margins. Legally, their rights were extremely limited, and they generally remained under the authority of their father (or brother) until their death. Financially, this meant they usually had to rely on the gracious financial support of male relatives or had to work harder to survive through jobs that provided a low income and low status.

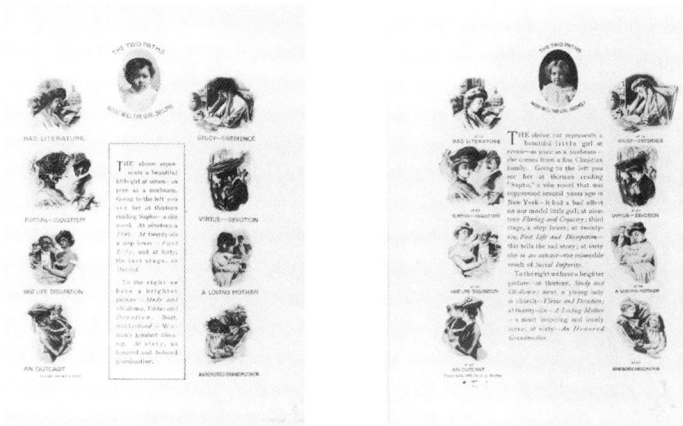

The Two Paths—What Will the Girl Become, 1903.
Courtesy of the Library of Congress.

These two images are each titled *The Two Paths—What Will the Girl Become* (1903). They serve as a warning: if a young girl focuses on her studies, being obedient and virtuous, she will become a mother and, even more rewarding, an honored grandmother. However, if she reads bad literature and enjoys flirting and going to parties, she will end up an outcast at the age of 40. It is inferred that the wrong path will cause women to miss out on marriage and motherhood—"woman's greatest blessing." This type of discourse isn't too different from the scare tactics aimed at single women today.

Additionally, there were times throughout history when governments enacted even harsher laws that specifically targeted unmarried and childless people, in an attempt to curb falling birth rates. Because of the limited availability and accessibility of resources outside of European texts, I am able to present this historical information only from a Western viewpoint. However, political regimes across history and civilizations have had an interest in controlling their population through pronatalist policies, with the goal of increasing the number of potential soldiers, workers (including slaves), and taxpayers.

As early as the first century BCE, the Roman Emperor Augustus enacted legislation that penalized unmarried or childless men and women. Unmarried people were forbidden from receiving inheritances; widows and widowers without children were deprived of part of their inheritance; and widows were expected to remarry within a year or two, after which they faced penalties.[4]

During the seventeenth century, the French King Louis XIV promulgated his Edict on Marriage (1666), which aimed to promote procreation by offering tax privileges to fathers of ten or more children. It also discouraged celibacy by raising the age required to join religious orders. Around the same time, in England, the Marriage Duty Act (1695) pressured people to marry and have children by taxing single men over the age of 25 and childless widowers.

Unmarried women were also specifically targeted at times, especially when they lived or worked independently, as they were then viewed as a threat to the patriarchy. For example, from the fifteenth to the seventeenth century, English towns regularly forbade single women to live alone or in a household that wasn't headed by a male. Some cities even threatened them with incarceration or expulsion.[5]

This overview of the multiple ways in which unmarried women have been mistreated is an important starting point in the study of the history of single women. However, it shouldn't be the only focus. Rather, we should aim to recognize the unique sociocultural position of single women in general and acknowledge the individual qualities of each woman, such as their resilience, intelligence, and innovative spirit, in order to honor their lives, accomplishments, and legacies.

Looking Backward, circa 1912, by Laura E. Foster. Courtesy of the Library of Congress.

The image on the previous page shows a woman looking back down a flight of stairs, which start with steps labeled "love," "marriage," and "children," then "career," "artistic success," "professional triumph," and at the very top "suffrage," "loneliness," "fame." Two happy children stand on the bottom steps, which are brimming with flowers, while the upper steps are bare and cracked. The scene and the woman's torn expression imply that women who pursue their ambitions—leaving behind the ideas of marriage, children, and the home—will eventually regret their choice.

Safe in Dangerous Waters, 1903, by Samuel Ehrhart. Captioned "the real American girl is too clever to be wrecked here." Courtesy of the Library of Congress.

Above: Because of the sunken "American fortunes" boats and the royal crown, it is likely a reference to the trend of wealthy American women who married into impoverished British aristocracy during the Gilded Age. Nonetheless, I like the imagery of this young woman confidently navigating a sailboat through the rocky and treacherous "sea of matrimony," without falling into the water or wrecking her ship.

A Short Chronology of Historical Achievements by Single Women

First famous female scientist whose life was recorded
Hypatia (c. 350–415)

First famous female composer in the West
Hildegard of Bingen (c. 1098–1179)

First known female Renaissance painter of Florence
Sister Plautilla Nelli (1524–1588)

First woman to study at a university in the Netherlands
Anna Maria van Schurman (1607–1678)

First woman to receive a PhD
Elena Piscopia (1646–1684)

The "First English Feminist"
Mary Astell (1666–1731)

First woman to write a mathematics handbook
Maria Gaetana Agnesi (1718–1799)

First known female astronomer to be paid for her work
Caroline Herschel (1750–1848)

First African American to be employed as a star route postwoman in the US
Mary Fields (c. 1832–1914)
a.k.a. "Stagecoach Mary"

First woman to win the Nobel Prize in Literature
Selma Lagerlöf (1858–1940)

First official White House photographer
Frances Benjamin Johnston (1864–1952)

First woman to obtain an architecture license in California
Julia Morgan (1872–1957)

First woman elected to the US Congress
Jeannette Rankin (1880–1973)

First woman to serve as
a state Supreme Court Justice
Florence Ellinwood Allen (1884–1966)

First woman to conduct major orchestras
Nadia Boulanger (1887–1979)

First female baseball umpire in the US
Amanda Clement (1888–1971)

First Latin American author to win
the Nobel Prize in Literature
Gabriela Mistral (1889–1957)

First Chinese American actress to gain
international recognition
Anna May Wong (1905–1961)

First woman to swim across
the English Channel
Gertrude Ederle (1905–2003)

First Native woman to work as
an engineer in the US space program
Mary G. Ross (1908–2008)

First woman to own a seat
on the New York Stock Exchange
Muriel Siebert (1928–2013)

First African American woman
to reach the North Pole
Barbara Hillary (1931–2019)

First woman to be awarded
the Pritzker Architecture Prize
Zaha Hadid (1950–2016)

CHAPTER 1

How single women have inspired me by

DEFYING TRADITIONAL GENDER NORMS THROUGHOUT ANCIENT HISTORY

Throughout history, young women have always been praised for their silence and submissiveness. Even today, it takes a certain amount of strength to challenge those expectations. This chapter is dedicated to women who, centuries before the first feminist movements, refused to be limited by the gender norms of their environment.

By remaining unmarried, whether by choice or by circumstances, single women everywhere—no matter their religion, culture, or social class—would have been seen as going against societal expectations. However, I want to emphasize how single women's defiance of gender norms could often go beyond their marital status: other acts of resistance were carried out, as varied and diverse as the women themselves.

Some women objected to one specific standard—such as the limits on women's education—while others rejected every single norm associated with traditional femininity: from the fact that women were discouraged from engaging in public discourse to the way that they were expected to dress, style their hair, and carry themselves. Some shared their journey very publicly, while others took action quietly, within their own home. Some could be considered rebellious by today's standards, while others might now seem too conformist to a modern audience. All defied gender norms in their own way.

There is something quite powerful to be found in the lives of these women, whether they initiated broad public actions or smaller intimate ones. Their stories have reinforced my own determination not to let my life be dictated by societal norms, especially those that relate to marriage, motherhood, and the idea of traditional femininity as it pertains to clothing, appearance, behaviors, and activities.

Gārgī Vāchaknavī

(c. seventh century BCE)
Inquisitive philosopher of ancient India

———————

Gārgī Vāchaknavī is one of the most notable female figures of the Vedic era. Her lasting legacy as a philosopher highlights her unique position and achievements in a male-dominated environment.

Born in ancient India, Gārgī Vāchaknavī was the daughter of the sage Vachaknu. This played a role in the education she received: she was encouraged to study the sacred texts of the Vedas (scriptures of Vedism, which predated Hinduism) and became quite knowledgeable in matters of philosophy and religion.

Intellectually gifted and descending from a long lineage of philosophers, she devoted herself to being a lifelong scholar, and for that reason, she never married. She earned the title of Brahmavadini, a woman who pursues the intellectual, religious, and philosophical studies of the highest order. This honorific title can be contrasted with that of Sadyovadhu, the wife and mother who focuses on domestic matters— although both are meant to honor and respect an idealized aspect of womanhood.

Vāchaknavī is especially remembered for her role in a philosophical debate that was held at the court of King Janaka of Videha during the seventh century BCE. The king had offered one thousand cows that were adorned with gold to the most knowledgeable of his guests. One man named Yajnavalkya—a scholar and priest— declared himself to be the obvious winner over everyone else. Among the crowd, only eight of the guests dared challenge him, including one woman, Vāchaknavī. The eight contestants each took turns debating philosophical questions with Yajnavalkya to try to disprove him. Interestingly, Vāchaknavī was the only one to question him twice, a fact that, along with her sex, set her apart from the others.

Even though Yajnavalkya remained undefeated and was officially declared the prize winner, Vāchaknavī's legacy was cemented by her distinctive role in the debate. Some have viewed her portrayal, which calls attention to the difference between her conduct and that of the male scholars, as a sign of women's inferiority to male philosophers. However, from a feminist perspective, her story can also be perceived as a sign of boldness, strength, intelligence, and uniqueness—as an example of a woman who rivaled male scholars, competing at equal level in public philosophical discourse.

Lady Triêu

(c. 225–248)
Warrior maiden who became a national symbol in Vietnam

Fueled by a desire to fight the oppression of her people, Lady Triêu defied traditional expectations by taking on the role of a warrior rather than a wife.

Orphaned at a young age, Lady Triêu (also known as Bà Triêu or by her full name, Triêu Thi Trinh) grew up living in her brother's household, where she suffered at the hands of her brother's cruel wife. In one version of her story, the situation became so bad that Triêu killed her sister-in-law in a desperate attempt to end the abuse.

As a young woman, Triêu openly rejected the idea of marriage, possibly because wives were required to submit to and serve their husbands. Instead, she wanted to resist foreign oppression and free her people, something she expressed in the following words:

"I want to ride the storm, tread the dangerous waves, [. . .]
Win back the Fatherland and destroy the yoke of slavery.
I do not want to bow down my head working as a simple housewife."[6]

At that time, the Vietnamese people were under the rule of the Chinese kingdom of Eastern Wu. At only 19, Trêu rallied over one thousand people to take arms against foreign domination. By the age of 21, she had led at least thirty battles. In 248, during one of those regional uprisings, Trêu and her army were defeated. Rather than surrender, she was said either to have died by suicide or to have been killed by her opponents. She was only 23 years old.

Her story, as told through centuries, is weaved from both facts and fiction. For instance, according to traditional lore, she rode into battle on an elephant. She was also portrayed, in embellished narratives, as being nine feet tall, with three-foot-long breasts that she carried over her shoulders. She remains nonetheless remembered for her courage and her outspoken desire to live outside the bounds of the traditional role of women. By fighting for her people, Triêu cemented a long-lasting legacy, serving as a national symbol of patriotism and inspiring generations of Vietnamese women to rise against oppressors, including French colonizers and American invaders of the twentieth century.

Hypatia

(c. 350–415)
Antiquity's defiant mathematician

———————

Hypatia was a mathematician, astronomer, and philosopher who, as a scholar and single woman in a male-dominated society, broke significant gender norms by teaching in public. Her decision to remain single allowed her to pursue her scholarly interests without the usual constraints of marriage.

Hypatia was born in Alexandria (Egypt) to an upper-class family. Her father was a renowned mathematician who ensured she would be provided with an advanced education. With his support, Hypatia grew to become profoundly knowledgeable in matters of mathematics, astronomy, and philosophy. She wrote commentaries on the works of previous mathematicians, such as the astronomer Apollonius of Perga and the algebra pioneer Diophantus, and was able to position herself as a respected scholar, which was highly unusual for women. Hypatia's father seemingly prided himself on his daughters' intellect, and they even worked together on a commentary of book 3 of the *Almagest*, written by the scientist Ptolemy.

She further pushed the boundaries of social convention by teaching in front of crowds of people at a time when public teaching was considered to be out of bounds for women. However, her reputation was such that both men and women came from afar to hear her talk.

In addition to her intellectual aptitudes, she was described by her biographers as having self-assurance and a composed manner. The philosopher Damascius even remarked, "Though, naturally modest and fair minded, she remained unwed."[7]

Singleness was most likely an advantageous path for Hypatia: she could devote herself to her studies and did not have to submit to the control of a husband. Even if, under the patriarchal system, she was always legally subjected to the authority of a male figure, since her father and brother were supportive of her endeavors and did not impede her work, she might have preferred to remain attached to them rather than risk marrying someone who could turn out to be conservative in their beliefs about gender roles.

As a pagan who lived in a Judeo-Christian environment, Hypatia faced some opposition from Christian officials. Because of rising religious and political tensions and because she had become a symbol of pagan and female scholarship, she was brutally murdered in 415 AD by religious zealots. This tragic end did not extinguish her legacy, and even today, she remains a well-known figure of early scientific women who accomplished remarkable feats.

Song Ruoshen and Song Ruozhao

(ninth century)
Influential Confucian scholars

————

Song Ruoshen (d. 820) and Song Ruozhao (d. 825) were two sisters who, despite the limitations placed on women, became scholars at the emperor's court, a public and influential role that they held for decades.

Song Ruoshen and Song Ruozhao were the two eldest of five daughters (and one son) born to the Confucian scholar Song Tingfen, who tutored them and encouraged their scholarly interests. Raised in China during the Tang dynasty (which lasted from 618 to 906), the sisters also descended from the poet Song Zhiwen, one of the most important poets of the reign of Empress Wu Zetian.

The five sisters (Ruoshen, Ruozhao, Ruoxian, Ruolun, and Ruoxun) became renowned for their intelligence as well as their beauty. In 788, they were invited to the imperial palace of Emperor Dezong, where their knowledge and aptitudes were tested. After showcasing their talent, the sisters were offered official positions at court and invited to perform poetry during festivities. They were treated like scholars and teachers, maintaining their position and presence at court for almost four decades, through the reigns of multiple emperors—an impressive feat!

Ruoshen and Ruozhao both had no interest in marriage, and, given their family's own impressive lineage, it might have been hard to find the perfect match. Remaining unmarried allowed them to focus on intellectual pursuits rather than be confined at home, under the authority of a husband. In that sense, they followed the path of Ban Zhao (c. 49–c. 120), the most famous female scholar in China, who was widowed young with a son and never remarried, preferring to devote her time to her work.

Among their scholarly contributions, Ruoshen wrote (and Ruozhao annotated) a manual for the conduct of women titled *The Analects for Women* (Nü lunyu), which supplemented Zhao's influential *Lessons for Women*. Despite their own unconventional life paths, these female scholars adhered to the Confucian views about the submissive role of women. However, at a time when women received little to no education, their work was progressive and trailblazing, which is further demonstrated by the fact that these educational treatises were read by upper-class women for centuries.

Wallada bint al-Mustakfi

(c. 994–c. 1091)

Free-spirited al-Andalus princess and poet

———

Wallada bint al-Mustakfi was a literary figure of al-Andalus, the Muslim-ruled region of Spain in the Middle Ages. To our modern eye, she exemplifies the ability to exercise autonomy and agency in an environment dictated by strict gender roles.

Raised in Córdoba, the multicultural and intellectual capital of al-Andalus, Wallada bint al-Mustakfi was the daughter Muhammad III, who briefly served as caliph of Córdoba from 1024 to 1025, during a politically tumultuous time. After his death in 1025, as the only heir, she inherited all of her father's fortune.

Of noble birth, educated, eloquent, and wealthy, al-Mustakfi established her own literary salon, where she welcomed men and women without any physical separation.

An independent spirit, she rebelled against most social conventions of the time: she walked around freely (rather than being confined inside, as was expected of upper-class women), refused to wear a veil, and rejected marriage. She was able to defy traditional norms so openly because of her high-ranking social status and privilege.

Confident and strong willed, she even embroidered on her clothes positive affirmations that were visible to everyone as she walked by. On one shoulder, she bore the following demonstration of self-esteem: "I am, by Allah, fit for high positions and am going my way, with pride!" while on the other, she boldly displayed her passionate nature with this statement: "I allow my lover to kiss my cheek and bestow my kisses on him who craves it."[8]

Al-Mustakfi was famed for her beauty and described as having blue eyes, red or blonde hair, and fair skin. She had a well-known love affair with Ibn Zaydun, one of the most prestigious poets of al-Andalus, and their story, which was passionate, dramatic, and scandalous, was immortalized in history and literature, including in her own verses in which she slanders him with obscene language, another example of her defiant attitude toward social conventions. Her legacy survived rather well, as centuries later, the Algerian-born historian Ahmed Mohammed al-Maqqari (1577–1632) wrote about how she was "unique in her time, endowed with gracious speech, lavishly praised."[9]

Hildegard of Bingen

(c. 1098–1179)

Mystic, theologian, composer, and healer

––––––––––

Leading a community of nuns in medieval Europe, Hildegard of Bingen defied gender norms by engaging publicly in activities typically reserved for men, such as theological writing and preaching.

Hildegard of Bingen was the youngest of ten children born into a noble German family. Because she had religious visions and also because of her fragile health (which might have limited future marriage prospects), she was dedicated to God during her childhood. She was entrusted to the care of Countess Jutta von Sponheim, a young noblewoman who was educated and pious and had no desire to be married. In 1112, when von Sponheim was enclosed inside a cell attached to the male monastery of Disibodenberg, Hildegard followed her into this ascetic lifestyle, officially joining religious orders at the age of 14.

Over the years, a community of around a dozen religiously devoted noblewomen formed under von Sponheim's influence. After von Sponheim's death in 1136, Hildegard, now 38 years old, was elected as the next leader of this small congregation. She thrived in that position and eventually left the monks of Disibodenberg to establish her own female monasteries: the monastery of Rupertsberg, near Bingen (in 1150), and then the monastery of Eibingen (in 1165). There, she was able to implement unconventional religious practices, such as during feast days, when her nuns wore long, white, floor-length silk veils and gold crowns adorned with crosses—bride-like garments that were somewhat ostentatious and went against the Christian ideals of poverty and (female) modesty.

At the age of 42, she received an instruction from God to put her visions in writing, which she did with the help of a monk named Volmar. At a time when the Church expected women to be submissive and silent, Hildegard's writings and public preaching received some opposition, which she navigated by stating that her education and knowledge were so limited that she was merely a vessel for the word of God. Her visions were recorded over multiple decades in three volumes called *Scivias*, *Liber Vitae Meritorum*, and *Liber Divinorum Operum*. She is also known for her treatise on healing herbs and natural medicine, her numerous musical compositions—for which she is considered the first identifiable female composer in the history of Western music—and her correspondence with prominent figures. Her life has inspired multiple biographies and a German movie, *Vision* (2009), directed by Margarethe von Trotta.

CHAPTER 2

What single women have taught me about

THE IMPORTANCE OF
FINANCIAL INDEPENDENCE

The subject of finances has always been central to women's lives. While today's financial advice focuses on investments, emergency funds, and retirement accounts, in the past, dowries and inheritances were the primary concerns.

Wealth—or lack of wealth, actually—shaped women's lives, especially in how it influenced their marriage prospects. Broadly speaking, women from the upper class were expected to marry for money or political power, while women from the lower class contributed to their husband's earnings with unpaid domestic labor, such as cooking, cleaning, and childbearing.

In most legal systems, a married woman also relinquished control of her finances to her husband. On the other hand, at least in common law systems, unmarried women could benefit from the status of feme sole, which allowed them to enter contracts, manage property, and engage in court proceedings—rights that were denied to married women. Remaining legally single could therefore seem much more appealing than marriage, and for good reason.

However, single women also faced a greater risk of being destitute, as their employment perspectives were limited and they did not benefit from the protections of mothers and widows. Nonetheless, the desire to be able to claim and manage their earnings, dowries, and inheritances could have factored in the decision of some women to remain single, especially those with an entrepreneurial spirit or a strong sense of agency.

In 2025, financial literacy is a popular topic, and self-sufficiency is considered essential because of the inherent danger of being reliant on anyone else, particularly a romantic partner, not only because of the risk of abuse but also because of the possibility of job loss, divorce, or death. But even in the past, single women were acutely aware of the legal ramifications of both marriage and singlehood, and for some marriage was too much of a financial risk.

Rosalba Carriera

(c. 1675–1757)
Prolific pastel portraitist

_____

Rosalba Carriera was able to achieve what many artists dream of: financial and artistic success—a notable accomplishment, especially for a woman of her time. Having independently established herself, she was reluctant to risk it all by marrying, which could mean losing control over her finances and her own aspirations as an artist.

Rosalba Carriera was born into a modest working-class family in Venice (Italy). She first started doing lace-making alongside her mother, but when it went out of fashion at the end of the seventeenth century, she turned to painting miniatures on the lids of tobacco boxes. These were bought as souvenirs by upper-class travelers, and her reputation quickly grew among this international crowd.

An established artist by 1700, Carriera became an honorary member of the Accademia di San Luca in 1705 and a member of the French Académie Royale de Peinture et de Sculpture in 1720. Her artistic style was defined by an exclusive use of pastels and has been associated with the Rococo art movement, known for its pastel colors and delicate (yet ornate) elements. She was an in-demand artist, and her commissions included portraits of Frederick IV of Denmark in 1709; the future Louis XV of France, as a child, around 1720; the French painter Antoine Watteau (considered the father of Rococo painting) in 1721; and the future Holy Roman Empress, Maria Theresa, in 1730. To complete the hundreds of pieces that were commissioned, she was assisted in her work by her younger sister, Giovanna, who also remained unmarried.

Later in life, Carriera acknowledged her indifference toward marriage: "My work, which keeps me too busy, and a natural coldness have always kept me far from suitors and thoughts of marriage. I would certainly make the world laugh if now, having already passed my youth, I entered into such things."[10] She conceded to prioritizing her work and brushed aside further questions of marriage by saying that she was simply too old now. This could have been a polite way to end the subject without admitting that she had remained single on purpose (which would have been inconceivable at the time). Being single allowed Carriera to have full control over her business and its financial success. Had she married, her husband would have been the one with the right to make final decisions—including possibly deciding to shut down the production. Given her thriving business and career, it's not surprising that she wasn't that interested in marriage.

Lady Elizabeth Hastings

(1682–1739)

Wealthy heiress and philanthropist

———

After Lady Elizabeth Hastings inherited her family's immense wealth in her early twenties, she rejected any marriage proposals, most likely to be able to safeguard her fortune. Instead, she focused on managing her wealth, philanthropic efforts, and supporting her female relatives.

Elizabeth Hastings was born into a wealthy aristocratic family in Great Britain, a privileged position in terms of social status, and it is likely she was considered an attractive marriage prospect by eligible men.

As the sole surviving descendant on her mother's side, she inherited her family's immense wealth in 1704, at the age of 22. She would have realized the freedom and independence that this financial security granted her, and it is possible that she chose not to marry in order to not lose control over her money, her family's properties, and her investments. She also had younger half sisters (from her father's second marriage) who needed her financial support and she might have been afraid that an ill-suited marriage could jeopardize her ability to help them.

Basically, instead of marriage being a path toward financial stability and social acceptance, marriage represented such a risk for Hastings that it was easier to bear the stigma of being a spinster. It's therefore unsurprising that she rejected multiple marriage proposals.

Hastings was well-connected and her circle included some other admirable women, such as Mary Astell, often called the first English feminist, who was also an advocate for women's education. Like Hastings, Astell remained unmarried, exploring the inequalities of marriage in *Some Reflections upon Marriage* (1700) and viewing singleness as an advantage, writing "the whole world is a single Lady's family, her opportunities of doing good are not lessen'd but encreas'd by her being unconfin'd."[11] In light of that statement, we can see how Hastings's philanthropic efforts were, if not increased, at the very least not limited by the traditional responsibilities that come with marriage and motherhood.

Hastings managed her wealth well, including by investing in the early stock market. She was also a significant charitable benefactor who helped fund educational projects. In her will, she provided annuities for her unmarried half sisters, to ensure their welfare, and also instituted the creation of scholarships and the Lady Elizabeth Hastings Charities, which continue to benefit students today.

Mary Moody Emerson

(1774–1863)

The great-aunt of transcendentalists

———

"[I] promised never to put that ring on."

As a spinster who was uninterested in marriage, Mary Moody Emerson's desire to be independent was fulfilled when she received an inheritance which allowed her to be financially secure and live on her own.

Mary Moody Emerson was born into a New England family that descended from the 1630s Puritans on both sides. She was only 2 years old when her father died. The youngest child, she was sent away from her mother and siblings to live with impoverished extended family. This difficult childhood likely shaped her resilience and desire for autonomy.

Mary Moody Emerson received little formal schooling, and after the age of 12, she was mostly self-taught. While the men in the Emerson family were sent to attend Harvard University, Emerson was not allowed any educational opportunities. To satisfy her intellectual curiosity, she read the classics in literature, philosophy, and history.

In 1791, at the age of 17, she began working in the households of various relatives, assisting them depending on their needs. This was not an unusual situation for unmarried women who—often viewed as a burden and another mouth to feed—were expected to provide domestic labor to alleviate the financial strain they represented and to fulfill their role as dutiful daughters.

Present in the lives of her nieces and nephews, she had a profound influence on her nephew Ralph Waldo Emerson, who would become known for his involvement in the transcendentalist philosophical movement.

In her thirties, Emerson's life changed when she received an inheritance, which she invested in a property in rural Maine where she could live alone. An independent spirit, she nonetheless maintained intellectual relationships with learned men and women through correspondence, including transcendentalists Elizabeth Peabody, Henry David Thoreau, and Amos Bronson Alcott (Louisa May Alcott's father).

From around 1802 to 1855, she wrote her *Almanacks*, over one thousand unpublished manuscript pages that offer precious insight into the life of an intellectual woman of the time. They also reflect her feelings on marriage, which were made quite clearly when she stated that she "promised never to put that ring on."[12]

Elleanor Eldridge

(1784–c. 1865)

Pragmatic entrepreneur and landowner

———

Born free at the end of the eighteenth century, Elleanor Eldridge was keenly aware of the obstacles she faced as an illiterate woman of color in a segregated society. Eager not to have to rely on anyone to secure her own future, she prioritized becoming self-sufficient, through hard work and profitable business endeavors.

Elleanor Eldridge was born free, in Rhode Island, to a family of African and Native American descent. Her paternal grandparents had been forcibly taken from Central Africa and enslaved in the US, but her father had earned his freedom by fighting in the American Revolution (1775–1783) and her mother was a free woman of mixed African and Narragansett (Native American) heritage.

Around the age of 10, after her mother's death, Eldridge was indentured to a local family, a common situation for poor orphans. She became an expert at weaving (a high-in-demand skill) as well as spinning, house painting, laundering, cheese making, and soapmaking In her late twenties, even though she was illiterate, she made use of those manual skills to start a business. With the profits, she acquired land. By 1827, she owned multiple properties, including rentals, and by 1838, she was one of the wealthiest people of color in her area.

In 1831 and 1832, she temporarily went out of state twice, first to recover from typhus fever, then to flee a localized cholera epidemic. Both times, rumors of her death started circulating, and her estate was fraudulently seized by a lender in compensation for unpaid loans. Eldridge filed a lawsuit in 1837 and worked with a local white woman, Frances Harriet Whipple, a women's rights activist and abolitionist, to raise money by transcribing her story in *Memoirs of Elleanor Eldridge* (1838). The book sold well and was followed by *Elleanor's Second Book* (1839), which detailed how she was eventually able to repurchase her property with an out-of-court settlement.

Eldridge never married. She claimed that her aunt had advised her against marriage, believing it was a waste of time. In a way, Eldridge seemed to agree with that when she stated, "While my young mistress was courting and marrying, I knit five pairs of stockings."[13] Remaining single also allowed her to enter contracts and own property—which was essential for her business dealings—whereas married women were unable to do so until legislation started changing in the late 1840s.

Annie Smith Peck

(1850–1935)
The scholarly mountaineer

———

"Years ago I made up my mind that I would never marry."

Determined not to let society's expectations get in her way, Annie Smith Peck carved her own path toward a career and financial independence. As a lecturer, she capitalized on her strengths—the combination of her scholarly knowledge and her thrilling adventures—to fascinate and educate audiences.

From a young age, Annie Smith Peck was determined never to marry. In 1874, in a letter to her father, she wrote, "Years ago I made up my mind that I would never marry and consequently that it would be desirable for me to get my living in the best possible way and to set about it as any boy would do."[14] Her intentions were clear: she wanted the same educational opportunity her brothers and her father had benefited from, one that could set her on a career path through which she could support herself financially.

In her mid-twenties, she enrolled at the University of Michigan, which had accepted its first female student in 1870. She graduated with a bachelor's degree in Greek in 1878, followed by a master's degree in 1881, and became a college professor herself, teaching Latin and elocution.

She then moved to Europe from 1884 to 1886 to study in Germany and Greece. During this time, she discovered mountain climbing, an increasingly popular activity. Peck became a skillful mountaineer, but in 1895, after climbing one of the highest summits in the Alps (the Matterhorn), her achievement was overshadowed by the scandal caused by her unconventional outfit; she had worn pants! Indeed, as senseless as it sounds today, female mountain climbers were expected to wear heavy and voluminous dresses, which were both uncomfortable and unsafe for such activities. Unbothered by the criticism, Peck continued mountaineering across Europe and challenged herself by climbing unclaimed peaks in South America.

By 1892, in her mid-forties, Peck made a comfortable living lecturing and writing about archaeology, mountain climbing, and her travels. A Pan-American expert, she promoted peace and cultural understanding across the Americas. She was also a proponent of women's rights, and when she climbed Mount Coropuna in Peru in 1911, at the age of 61, she planted a sign at the summit that read: "Votes for Women." She completed her last climb at the age of 82 and even started another world tour at the age of 84, in 1935. Unfortunately, she fell ill and died from pneumonia.

Teresa de la Parra

(1889–1936)
Venezuelan novelist and social critic

In her work as a writer and lecturer, Teresa de la Parra viewed financial independence as essential to women's lives, a way to escape submission to the patriarchy (such as the pressure to marry for money and security); she herself experienced this liberation when she became independently wealthy via an inheritance.

Born into a wealthy Venezuelan family, Teresa de la Parra lived in Europe during her preteen and teen years, returning to Venezuela only as a young adult, around the age of 20. Drawing inspiration from her own experience, she wrote her first novel, *Iphigenia: Diary of a Young Girl Who Wrote Because She Was Bored* (1924), which tells the story of a young woman who, after being raised in France and following the death of her father, returns to Caracas at the age of 18. Yearning for freedom but financially dependent on the generosity of her extended family, she struggles to adapt to the strict moral and social rules of Caracas society.

Titled after the sacrifice of Iphigenia in Greek mythology, the novel surrenders its heroine to a loveless (but financially advantageous) marriage. Despite some outcry from conservatives, the book was a success.

Contrary to her heroine in *Iphigenia*, de la Parra herself never married, although she has been linked to both the male Ecuadorian writer Gonzalo Zaldumbide as well as the female Cuban writer Lydia Cabrera, her companion in her last years.

While she had earned money from her writing, de la Parra's own financial situation completely changed in her mid-thirties when, in 1924, she inherited the estate of her childless friend and mentor, Emilia Ibarra. This event reshaped her future, as this newfound wealth allowed her to be freed from the financial pressures faced by many women, some of which she had criticized in *Iphigenia*. She was able to fully focus on her writing, research, and lectures, and she published her second book, *Mama Blanca's Memoirs*, in 1929.

De la Parra viewed financial independence as a necessary tool for women's emancipation: in a 1930 speech, she spoke of the "dignity of women through financial independence and work"[15] and mentioned her contemporary Gabriela Mistral—the Chilean poet, educator, and diplomat—as representing that ideal. Unfortunately, de la Parra's own work was interrupted after she was diagnosed with tuberculosis, from which she passed away in 1936, at the age of 46.

Dorothy Shaver

(1893–1959)
The first woman to head a Fifth Avenue
department store

———

Dorothy Shaver's path to financial success was not linear. She was fired as a teacher for attending a dance without a chaperone, sold handmade dolls crafted by her sister, and worked in a department store where, with an eye for emerging trends and great business acumen, she climbed the corporate ladder, eventually becoming the first woman to lead a department store on one of New York's most prestigious avenues.

Dorothy Shaver was born to an affluent and respected family in rural Arkansas. She attended the University of Arkansas from 1911 to 1913 and worked as a schoolteacher until she was dismissed for attending a dance as a single woman without a chaperone in 1914.

In 1917, she moved to New York City with her sister Elsie. The two sisters started a successful business selling rag dolls made by Elsie, which were eventually sold by the upscale department store Lord & Taylor, whose president, Samuel Reyburn, was a distant relative of the Shaver sisters.

Starting in 1921, and for the next thirty-five years, Dorothy Shaver worked directly for Lord & Taylor. She rose rapidly to leadership positions: she became a director on the board in 1927, a vice president in 1931, first vice president in 1937, and president in 1945.

As the president of Lord & Taylor from 1945 to 1959, she was the first woman to head a Fifth Avenue department store. Although her salary, which was over $100,000 (over $1.4 million today), was the highest recorded for a woman at the time, it was still much less than her male equivalents were paid.

Nicknamed the "First Lady of Retailing," she is remembered for establishing the "American Look" in the 1930s. At the time, fashion trends worldwide were set by designers in Paris. Shaver's idea to hire American designers and promote their designs (through events, awards, and in-store setups) was innovative and a success. She was also one of the founding members, alongside Edith Head, Elizabeth Arden, and Helene Rubinstein, of the Fashion Group (a networking organization for women) in 1930. An active philanthropist, she received numerous honorary degrees, honors, and awards throughout her life.

Shaver never married and lived with her sister in a duplex penthouse apartment in Manhattan, enjoying the New York glamour and glitz that appeal to so many.

Dr. May Edward Chinn

(1896–1980)
Driven and self-reliant physician

"I was so dead set against getting married."

Having witnessed her mother's difficult life, shaped by long hours of arduous labor, and her father's inability to provide financially, May Edward Chinn's vision of marriage was not a happy one. By remaining single, she avoided many of the burdens and financial worries that had affected her mother.

May Edward Chinn was born to parents of mixed African American and Native American heritage in the US. Her mother, who worked low-paying jobs, had been able to send her to boarding school by secretly saving money. Unfortunately, Chinn contracted a serious jaw infection. It required multiple surgeries, and she had to return home.

In 1917, she enrolled at Columbia University's Teachers College to study music. During the Harlem Renaissance, in the early 1920s, she played piano as accompaniment to the singer Paul Robeson, before his rise to fame. Although she aspired to perform and teach piano as a career, she was discouraged by the discrimination she faced as a woman of color. Encouraged to switch to the field of science by one of her professors, she then became the first African American woman to graduate from Bellevue Hospital Medical College in 1926.

As a Black woman in medicine (a male-dominated field), she faced many obstacles as a result of both sexism and racial discrimination, but she persevered. Looking back at her experience at that time, she recounted in an interview with the *New York Times*: "I was 30 years old. I had fought hard to get to where was, but where was I? Interns did not get paid, so my mother had to continue working. [...] She was working at night, cleaning office buildings. I had tried to keep from blaming my father for my mother's condition, but I found myself blaming him anyway. I began to let myself wonder if this bitterness explained in part why I was so dead set against getting married."[16] It was, in part, her father's struggles with alcohol and unemployment that deterred her from marriage. Despite multiple proposals, she continuously refused to marry.

After studying with the inventor of the Pap smear test, she joined the Strang clinic, which focused on early cancer detection. She worked there from 1944 until her retirement in 1974. A well-known figure in Harlem, she found recognition nationally after the publication of her profile in the *New York Times* in 1979.

Maurine Dallas Watkins

(c. 1898–1969)

The million-dollar *Chicago* playwright

Maurine Dallas Watkins was a gifted playwright who, after finding nationwide success and praise with her play *Chicago*, left her job as a screenwriter to enjoy her life without the pressures of the entertainment industry or the public's scrutiny. Being independently wealthy freed her from most societal constraints and she remained single, traveled, and lived life on her own terms. Quite the dream!

Maurine Dallas Watkins was recognized for her writing potential at a young age. A top student throughout high school and college, she graduated from Butler University in 1919 and attended a playwright workshop by renowned drama professor George Pierce Baker at Radcliffe College.

In 1924, while working as a journalist for the *Chicago Tribune*, she reported on women who were accused of murder, such as Beulah Annan (a married woman who shot her affair partner, claiming he was an intruder, and later declared she was pregnant, although no birth was recorded) and Belva Gaertner (who shot her lover after an alcohol-fueled night in various jazz clubs and claimed she could not remember what had happened). Both were acquitted.

In 1926, while attending the Yale School of Drama, Watkins wrote a play inspired by the accused murderesses from Chicago that debuted on Broadway in 1926 under the name *Chicago*. An immediate success, it was later adapted as the 1927 film *Chicago* (produced by Cecil B. DeMille) and the 1942 film *Roxie Hart* (starring Ginger Rogers). After the latter's mild reception, Watkins refused to allow for further adaptations.

During the 1930s, Watkins worked as a screenplay writer in Los Angeles. She worked on some well-received movies but never re-created the success of her best-known work. Eventually, she left the entertainment industry; after all, she had earned enough money from *Chicago* that she would never need to work again. Instead, she invested her wealth in stocks, bought luxury items, and traveled the world. Little is known of her life after she disappeared from the public's view in the 1940s, but at the time of her death, her estate was valued at $2 million (over $14 million in today's dollars).

After her death in 1969, her estate sold the rights of *Chicago* to Bob Fosse and Gwen Verdon, which led to the Tony Award–winning Broadway musical *Chicago* (1975, 1996) and its Oscar-winning adaptation in 2002, enhancing Watkins's own legacy in the creative arts.

CHAPTER 3

How single women have reclaimed their lives by

PRIORITIZING PURSUITS OTHER THAN MARRIAGE

Being passionate about something—whether it's art, literature, science, or sports—often requires us to prioritize other tasks and activities. For women who are intent on pursuing time-demanding passions, the responsibilities that come with marriage (and motherhood) represent additional constraints that need to be carefully considered.

While many women today struggle with "having it all," this pressure isn't new. In the early sixteenth century, a promising young humanist named Alessandra Scala (1475–1506) asked her mentor: "Shall I marry, or devote my life to study?"[17] This simple question illustrates her awareness that marriage was likely not compatible with intellectual pursuits. Case in point, many talented women faded away from public view after marrying; in the lower social classes, they were occupied by domestic duties and work, while in the upper class, they managed the household and were expected to remain out of the male-dominated spheres to maintain their respectability.

Since it was more acceptable for unmarried women to engage with men as professionals or peers, women who aspired to become musicians, artists, writers, athletes, or public speakers might have chosen to remain single to preserve their ability to participate in these male-dominated activities.

The women in this chapter were fueled by their passion; they needed the space, liberty, and time to unleash their creativity. Many of them purposefully chose the single life because it offered them the necessary environment to pursue their interests.

Isotta Nogarola

(1418–1466)
Secluded Renaissance humanist

———

One of the most renowned women writers of the Italian Renaissance, Isotta Nogarola could have—like many of her talented contemporaries—faded from the public sphere had she married. However, with the support of her family and the praise of admirers, she made the choice to remain unmarried in order to prioritize her intellectual and literary work.

Isotta Nogarola was born into a noble and wealthy family during the Italian Renaissance, a time of intellectual and cultural flourishing. Her aunt, Angela Nogarola, was an acclaimed humanist poet, and her parents valued their daughters' education, as both Isotta and her sister, Ginevra, mastered Latin in their teens and exchanged correspondence with prominent humanists.

Given her age, social status, and family lineage, she would have been expected to marry. But she never did. She even declined at least one marriage proposal in 1453. Her decision not to marry might have been influenced by her desire to remain an active participant in the literary world. Indeed, married women were expected to focus on household matters and childbearing, forgoing their artistic or scholarly work. Nogarola even saw it happen to her own sister, Ginevra, after she married in 1438 and faded away from scholarly pursuits.

Circumventing the usual paths of either marriage or the convent, Nogarola chose to remain single to focus on her work; she studied ancient Greek and Roman philosophers as well as medieval Christian and Islamic scholars.

Because she was an unmarried woman who engaged publicly with men through her writing, Nogarola was attacked anonymously with false claims of incest in 1439. Although she was ardently defended by her supporters, these severe accusations profoundly affected her.

At a time when women were seen as inferior to men, Nogarola defended women by emphasizing the legacy of the Greek poet Sappho; the political and cultural influence in Rome of Cornelia, mother of the Gracchi; and the skilled eloquence of the Roman orator Hortensia. In her most famous work, *De pari aut impari Evae atque Adae peccato* (Of the Equal or Unequal Sin of Adam and Eve; 1451), she argued that if Eve was to be perceived as weaker and inferior to Adam, then Eve's sin would therefore have to be considered lesser—not worse—than Adam's.

Mihrî Hatun

(c. 1460–c. 1506)
Passionate Ottoman poet

———————

Remembered as one of the most influential women poets of her century, Mihrî Hatun's decision to remain single shaped her literary life, empowering her to carve out a space for herself in a male-dominated society.

Mihrî Hatun (also spelled "Khatun") was born in modern-day Türkiye, in the small but influential town of Amasya, an intellectual and cultural center of the Ottoman Empire. Her education, which was fostered by her father, went beyond the traditionally limited female education; she became well versed in sciences, literature, and Islamic law, as well as Arab and Persian languages.

With the combination of her family's high social status and her own talent, she was welcomed within the literary circle of Prince Ahmed, who was the son of the sultan and the governor of Amasya from around 1481 to 1513.

A gifted poet, Hatun is one of only three women who are mentioned alongside hundreds of male Ottoman poets in the sixteenth century *tezkires* (bibliographical dictionaries), the two others being Zeynep Hatun (d. 1474) and Ayşe Hubbi Hatun (d. 1590). In comparison to her contemporary Zeynep Hatun, who stopped composing poetry after she married, Hatun herself never married and never stopped writing. This unusual choice to remain single allowed her a certain freedom from the social restrictions that married women were subject to.

In her poems, Hatun wrote about love. While her virtuous reputation was never questioned by her biographers, she has been linked—possibly romantically—to several prominent men of the time. Her verses exude with the passion and desire of a lover: "At one glance / I loved you / With a thousand hearts / They can hold against me / No sin except my love for you / Come to me / Don't go away / Let the zealots think / Loving is sinful / Never mind / Let me burn in the hellfire / Of that sin."[18] In one of her most famous verses, Hatun criticizes the hadith (Islamic guidance), which states that women are deficient in reason, by countering "since they say women lack reason, all their words should be excused," implying that she could therefore not be blamed for making the claim that "a capable woman is much better than a thousand incapable men."[19]

Her talent was recognized at the highest level, and she received substantial monetary gifts from the sultan for her poetry. More than a hundred years after her death, she was mentioned by the famous Turkish explorer Evliya Çelebi, and in 1985, a crater on Venus was named Khatun in her honor.

Elena Lucrezia Cornaro Piscopia

(1646–1684)

The quiet rebellion of a young woman

Raised in an aristocratic environment that offered only two choices, marriage or the convent, Elena Cornaro Piscopia rejected the first and was denied the second. She rebelled quietly, in a way that was invisible to others, by taking religious vows in secret and wearing religious garments under her normal clothing.

Elena Cornaro Piscopia was born in the Republic of Venice (Italy) to parents who were unmarried and came from completely opposite social and economic backgrounds. Her father, who hailed from a prestigious, aristocratic Venetian family, eventually married her mother, purchased expensive nobility titles for his sons, and tried to have all his children be recognized as legitimate. But Piscopia's social and legal status among the nobility remained tarnished by her illegitimate birth. Perhaps experiencing firsthand the senseless rigidity of the social order prompted her to feel detached from its principles rather than dutiful toward them.

At a time when women barely received any education, Piscopia was privately tutored in the humanities (philosophy, theology), science, music, fine arts, and languages (Greek, Latin, French, Spanish, English, Hebrew, and Arabic). She became admired for her intellect and exchanged correspondence with scholars, political figures, and even royalty. Her scholarly abilities were such that in 1678, at the age of 32, she received a Doctorate of Philosophy from the University of Padua, for which she is considered to have been the first woman in the Western world to have earned a PhD degree.

In an attempt to improve her social status, her father tried to arrange a marriage without her knowledge or consent. She refused, stating that she had vowed herself to chastity since the age of 11. Disregarding her wishes, her father prohibited her from joining a convent and even obtained an exemption from the Pope to release her from her vows so that she would marry, but she persisted in her rejection of marriage.

At 19, in the presence of a clergyman, she privately dedicated herself to God. Outwardly, she lived the life of an upper-class woman, but she behaved as if she were a nun and even wore religious garments under her regular clothes. Her actions might not have been grandiose, but they allowed her to defy the patriarchal expectations placed on her.

Marie-Marguerite Biheron

(1719–1795)
Inventive anatomist

———————

Marie-Marguerite Biheron combined her interest in anatomy with her artistic talent to craft intricate wax anatomical models. At the time, these were an essential tool to study the human body, and she gained praise and recognition across France and neighboring countries for her pioneering work.

Marie-Marguerite Biheron, also known as Marie-Catherine Biheron, was born in France. Her father was an apothecary, and although he died during her childhood, he might have introduced her to his work, which could have fueled her initial interest in the medicinal field.

During her youth, Biheron took drawing lessons with the renowned Mademoiselle Madeleine Françoise Basseporte, a botanical illustrator and the first woman to serve as official painter of the royal botanical garden in 1741, during the reign of King Louis XV. Basseporte herself remained unmarried her whole life: she devoted herself to her career and was respected by major botanists of her time such as Bernard de Jussieu and Carl Linnaeus. This positive perspective on what life could be like for a single woman of great acclaim could have inspired Biheron to consider pursuing the same path.

After studying human dissection—informally since formal higher education was not open to women—Biheron became drawn to artificial anatomy and started crafting anatomical models made of wax. Her precision and technique rendered the pieces so accurate and lifelike that her work was presented to the French Academy of Sciences in 1759, in 1770, and in 1771 (a demonstration that King Gustav III of Sweden himself attended).

Although she earned only a modest living by hosting demonstrations and classes in her workshop in Paris, she did have notable visitors, such as the famed educator Madame de Genlis and the renowned philosopher Denis Diderot, who sent his own daughter to study women's anatomy and specifically childbirth with Biheron.

Her reputation extended abroad: she met and corresponded with Benjamin Franklin and traveled to London to exhibit her models. One of her anatomical sets was even acquired by Catherine the Great, empress of Russia, after a recommendation from Diderot to the queen.

Despite the limitations placed on women, Biheron carved a space for herself, combining her scientific and artistic interests into a sustainable endeavor through which she could maintain her independence as a single woman.

Jane Austen

(1775–1817)
Emblematic novelist of the Regency era

———————

Jane Austen's novels, which have captivated readers for generations, are known for depicting the conflicts between personal desires and societal expectations. Austen personally experienced this herself when she refused to settle into a financially advantageous marriage, preferring instead to pursue her writing with unrestricted freedom.

Born into a modest but respectable British family, Jane Austen started writing at a young age. Her characters and the themes explored in her best-known works—such as issues of social class, love, marriage, and gender roles—were inspired by her own circumstances. When she was around 20 years old, Austen met a young man named Tom Lefroy, who came from a family of high social standing and would later become lord chief justice of Ireland. There was mutual affection between them, but any possible romance would have been hindered by the fact that he was expected to marry well and wealthy, while Austen had no money and no dowry. A few years later, in 1802, Austen was proposed to by a well-off family friend. While at first, she accepted his proposal, the very next day, she broke the engagement for unknown reasons.

Her decision to remain single rather than settle and conform was probably driven by multiple factors, including wanting to remain in charge of her own time—which she could then devote to writing. Furthermore, even if she was very fond of her nieces and nephews, Austen knew multiple women who had died following childbirth, and she might have wanted to avoiding pregnancy because of the high risk of maternal mortality.

As unmarried women, Austen and her older sister Cassandra were dependent on their father and, after his death in 1805, on the goodwill of their brothers. Austen was well aware of the financial weight and social stigma that came with her decision to be an "old maid," but she must have felt compelled to bear those difficulties in order to be true to herself.

Her path to become a recognized writer wasn't straightforward: her first submission to a publisher was returned unopened, and after that, she had to publish her work anonymously and on commission, meaning she shouldered the costs herself. Nonetheless, her novels *Sense and Sensibility* (1811), *Pride and Prejudice* (1813), and *Mansfield Park* (1814) quickly became bestsellers, granting her a level of acclaim that still persists today.

Florence Nightingale

(1820–1910)
The Lady with the Lamp

"I don't know what a wife and mother feels and I am very glad I don't."

Florence Nightingale was a pioneering British nurse who decided early on to devote her life to caregiving, eschewing marriage and motherhood. Because of her interest in data analysis, she ushered nursing into a science-based discipline.

Born into a wealthy and philanthropic British family, Florence Nightingale's path toward being a nurse started during her youth, with visits to the poor and sick as well as caring for ill family members. After her sister's almost fatal illness in 1836 and the 1837 influenza epidemic, Nightingale felt a call from God to devote herself to caring for others.

Because of this religious devotion to her work, she refused at least two marriage proposals. Nightingale's former governess had died in childbirth, which might have also prompted her to reflect on the potentially deadly consequences of motherhood. She might also have been influenced, in a positive way, by the lives of two unmarried aunts, Julia and Martha Frances Smith, who were radical supporters of progressive causes (such as abolitionism and women's rights) and acquainted with notable figures such as the writer Helen Maria Williams and the scientist Mary Somerville.

Nightingale rose to fame during the Crimean War (1853–1856) when she was deployed to modern-day Istanbul (Türkiye). Making the rounds at night and looking over injured soldiers, she became known as the "Lady with the Lamp." After realizing that more soldiers were dying from infections than in battle, she advocated for better sanitary conditions and designed the coxcomb, a complex data visualization pie chart, to support her theories. She went on to found the first nursing school in the world, the Nightingale Training School for Nurses, which opened in 1860 to provide nurses with scientific and practical training.

Nightingale protested the contempt she faced as a single, childless woman, writing: "People often say to me, you don't know what a wife and mother feels. No, I say, I don't. And I am very glad I don't. And they don't know what I feel. [...] Let each person tell the truth from his own experience."[20] For some single women today, these words still ring true, as their point of view is often dismissed. However, as Nightingale states, there is value in everyone's unique life experience.

Mary Cassatt

(1844–1926)
Impressionist painter

"I am independent! I can live alone and I love to work."[21]

Mary Cassatt belonged to a generation of American women who increasingly voiced their desire to be freed from the rigid social conventions placed on women. Knowing that if she became a wife, she would be expected to give up her burgeoning career as a painter, she chose to remain single so that she could continue painting at a professional level.

Born to affluent American parents, Mary Cassatt spent a few years of her childhood in Europe, where she and her siblings were introduced to foreign languages, culture, and art museums, an experience that might have contributed to Cassatt's desire to become an artist herself. In 1860, at only 16, she began studies at the Pennsylvania Academy of the Fine Arts. A few years later, in 1866, against her father's wishes but with her mother's support, she moved to Paris to further her artistic training; there, because women couldn't attend the prestigious École des Beaux-Arts, she took private lessons from renowned male artists and practiced her skills at the Louvre Museum daily.

Despite growing critical praise, she struggled to establish herself: back home in the US, she faced difficulties finding customers to buy her work, she lost some paintings in the Great Chicago Fire of 1871, and since her father refused to provide any financial help, she almost gave up on pursuing art as a career. However, when she returned to Paris in 1874, she was invited by Edgar Degas to join a group of upcoming artists who had created their own independent exhibition after their work had been rejected by the official art exhibition of Paris. They would become known as the Impressionists and would revolutionize the artistic world with an innovative style that didn't follow the rules of classical art.

Cassatt herself became especially recognized for her tender portraits of mothers and children, even though she never married or had children. However, it is a testament to her own talent and ability to capture the emotions of her subjects.

Cassatt's desire to be an artist surpassed any inclination she might have had for marriage. In her own entourage, her sister Lydia and a few of her cousins also remained unmarried. This generation of American women identified with the "New Woman" ideal, which described feminist, educated, and independent career women— not unlike many women today.

Edmonia Lewis

(c. 1844–1907)

Relentlessly determined African American sculptor

———

Edmonia Lewis was a talented sculptor who defied expectations by moving abroad as a single woman, supporting herself as a working artist, and paying tribute to her mixed-race heritage in her sculptures. Focused as she was on her artistic pursuits, marriage was not a priority for her.

Edmonia Lewis was born to an African American father and a Native American mother. After the death of both her parents during her childhood, she was raised by maternal aunts in a Native American community in western New York.

In 1859, she enrolled at Oberlin College, the first institution of higher education to accept women and people of color in the US. During her studies, she was falsely accused of poisoning two white girls. After a trial during which she was acquitted, she was denied permission to graduate. She was also attacked one night by unknown assailants and left for dead. Fragilized and worn out by these aggressions and injustices, she struggled to find her place.

Lewis was advised by famous abolitionist Frederick Douglass to move east, possibly to find a more diverse and accepting city where she could flourish as an artist. She established herself as a professional sculptor in Boston in 1864 and settled in Rome in 1865, where she joined a vibrant community of American artists. There, she became acquainted with the circle of the lesbian actress Charlotte Cushman, which abounded with creative women. Although we have no knowledge of Lewis's private life, if she had been romantically involved with women, she would have encountered an additional barrier on top of her race and gender: her sexual identity.

Renowned for her neoclassical style, Lewis's sculptures often centered around themes related to Black or Indigenous people, such as *Forever Free* (1867), one of her most notable works, which celebrates the emancipation of enslaved people. She also sculpted portraits of prominent figures, such as the poet Phillis Wheatley and the former president Abraham Lincoln. In the late 1880s, the popularity of neoclassicism declined, and Lewis faded from the public sphere. Despite the obstacles she faced, she was the first American woman of color to achieve international recognition as a sculptor.

Tsuda Umeko

(1864–1929)
University founder

———

"I want to have my school, and never marry."

After spending her formative years in the US, Tsuda Umeko returned to her country of origin, Japan, and found herself stuck in between two cultures. She rejected the traditional path of marriage to focus on women's education.

Tsuda Umeko was born in Japan to a family that descended from samurai. Her father was a proponent of Japan's Westernization and volunteered his daughter for the Iwakura Mission, a long-term international diplomatic mission during which Japanese girls were sent abroad for education and cultural enrichment. Tsuda remained in the US for over ten years, from the age of 7 to 18. She received a standard American education and lived in the home of an older childless couple, Charles and Adeline Lanman, with whom she remained in contact her whole life.

Away from her family of origin, Tsuda bonded with two compatriots who were also part of the mission, Shige Nagai and Sutematsu Yamakawa. Upon their return to Japan, the three young women hoped to be able to find suitable work. Unfortunately, the government had no interest in these overeducated women. Disappointed, her two friends both married and abandoned the pursuit of a career. However, Tsuda decided to become a teacher. In accordance with traditional Japanese education, she taught girls of the upper class how to become good wives and wise mothers. Yearning to do more, she raised money to establish a scholarship to help Japanese women receive higher education in the US.

Tsuda's main purpose was her work, and she admonished those who kept pressuring her to marry, stating: "Please don't write marriage to me again—not once. [. . .] I want to have my school, and never marry."[22] She also recognized the prejudice she faced as a single woman, lamenting: "Oh, it is so hard to feel yourself as different from others, and be looked on with contempt! If I could only do my own way, and not have everybody think me strange, just because I am not married."[23]

In 1900, she opened a higher-education institution, which still operates today as Tsuda University, and in 1902, she became legally independent from her father. Even though she had strong ties to the US and had met notable figures such as the activist Helen Keller and Eleanor Roosevelt, her legacy in Western countries was mostly forgotten until the first biography in English, by Yoshiko Furuki in 1991.

Marie Marvingt

(1875–1963)
Fiancée du Danger

"If I had been married, I could certainly never have lived the life I've lived."

Nicknamed the "Fiancée du Danger" because of her fearless attitude, Marie Marvingt was a Red Cross nurse, French Resistance hero, public speaker, journalist, record-breaking athlete, and aviation pioneer—an unusually wide-ranging set of interests and skills that earned her international acclaim and awards.

Born in the French countryside, Marie Marvingt was encouraged by her father to pursue athletic activities at a young age. During her life, she tried out almost every sport, winning first prizes and breaking records along the way, especially in swimming, mountain climbing, and bicycling. Most notably, she was the first woman to (unofficially) complete the Tour de France in 1908! Because women were not allowed to participate, she rode behind the men, outperforming 78 of the 114 male participants who dropped out before the end of the race.

She was also one of the first women in aviation. She learned to fly hot air balloons, airplanes, and helicopters and even invented a type of airplane-ambulance to lift injured soldiers out of war zones. A talented public speaker and polyglot, she promoted aeromedical evacuation at over six thousand conferences across the world (including one with Amelia Earhart in Chicago in 1935).

Marvingt inspired the American film series *The Perils of Pauline* (1914), which follows an independent young woman who yearns for adventurous experiences before marriage. Marvingt herself never married, stating: "I will never marry. I couldn't bear the ties of marriage [. . .] Climbing mountains is a lot more interesting to me than washing dishes."[24] In 1934, to highlight the fact that women are worthy of more than being known as just the "wives of," she wrote an article about the achievements of women married to famous men.

In 1958, looking back at her life, she expressed no regrets about remaining unmarried: "If I had been married, I could certainly never have lived the life I've lived, done the things I've done. I've not been just a sportswoman [. . .] I invented the ambulance-airplane, I fought at the front, I've tried to be useful in all circumstances."[25] For her achievements in various fields, she received thirty-four decorations, including the highest decoration in France, the Legion of Honor. Recent works, such as Rosalie Maggio's biography, *Marie Marvingt, Fiancée of Danger* (2019), have helped raise awareness of her fascinating story and bold personality.

Anna May Wong

(1905–1961)

Hollywood star and fashion icon

————

"I am wedded to my art,"[26] declared Anna May Wong, the first Chinese American Hollywood star, who followed her dream and pursued career opportunities across the world, moving as needed to find the best chances of success.

Born in Los Angeles to parents of Chinese lineage, Anna May Wong became fascinated by Hollywood's movie industry at a young age. She loved to watch film crews in the streets and even skipped school to go to the movies. She got her first role as an extra at the age of 14 and her first success at 17 with *The Toll of the Sea* (1922), an adaptation of the *Madame Butterfly* opera.

Unfortunately, her work opportunities were hindered by racism, sexism, and xenophobia. She struggled her whole life with being typecast as either a dangerous "Dragon Lady" or an innocent "Lotus Flower," but never a leading lady. This was exacerbated by the prohibition of interracial romance, which further limited the roles available to her. When the movie adaptation of Pearl Buck's novel *The Good Earth* (1931) was announced in 1935, Wong was considered for one of the principal roles. However, even though the story centers on a Chinese family in China, the leading roles went to Caucasian actresses who wore yellowface.

In her personal life, Wong was romantically linked to a few prominent white men from the movie industry (such as the cinematographer Charles Rosher). However, because anti-miscegenation laws prohibited interracial marriage, it would not have been possible to marry them even if she had wanted to. She also rejected the idea of a traditional Chinese marriage, which she felt would be too restrictive because of traditional gender norms.

Regardless, being single allowed her to chase opportunities wherever they arose, even if it meant moving across the ocean. In the late 1920s, frustrated with the entertainment industry in the US, Wong left for Europe; she found acclaim in Germany (where she befriended Marlene Dietrich), England (where she performed in the theater play *The Circle of Chalk* with Laurence Olivier and Rose Quong), and France. In 1936, she traveled for the first time to China, where she stayed close to a year, chronicling her experience for American newspapers. She returned to the US, and although her career stalled by the 1940s, she still made appearances in B movies and on early television, with her last on-screen appearance in 1961, the year of her death.

Keiko Fukuda

(1913–2013)
First woman to reach the highest ranks of judo

———

"I chose judo over marriage."

A tireless and determined spirit, Keiko Fukuda went against societal expectations and her family's desires by rejecting marriage and pursuing her true passion: judo.

Born into Japanese upper class, Keiko Fukuda was the granddaughter of a former samurai and a renowned jiujitsu master, Fukuda Hachinosuke. Her grandfather had trained the founder of judo, Kanō Jigorō, who personally invited Fukuda to join the women's judo classes in 1935. Fukuda was then 21, and her family expected her to marry. Fukuda, however, had no interest in marrying and becoming a housewife: "I didn't want to marry. I was obsessed with judo."[27] Her passion moved her to become a judo instructor in 1937. By 1953, she was promoted to the rank of fifth dan, the highest rank available to women at the time, and in 1964, she performed at the opening ceremony of the Tokyo Olympic Games.

Fukuda emigrated to the US in 1966 and lived in the San Francisco Bay Area with one of her students, Dr. Shelley Fernandez, who campaigned for Fukuda's promotion beyond fifth dan and for the recognition of her achievements in judo. In 1972, Fukuda became the first woman to reach sixth dan. Later on, she would be outranked by only three men, who had all started judo practice a decade later than she had. It was only after those men were promoted to the highest level of tenth dan that Fukuda reached the ninth dan, in 2006. While she was never awarded the tenth dan by the worldwide headquarters in Japan, USA Judo did grant her that honor in 2011.

The year before her death, the documentary *Mrs. Judo: Be Strong, Be Gentle, Be Beautiful* (2012), by Yuriko Gamo Romer, was released. As Fukuda recounts her life, her all-encompassing passion for judo is evident, but so are the sacrifices that came with it, such as when Fukuda tearfully reflects on the fact that she "chose judo over marriage."[28] To the viewer, her dedication to the discipline is nothing short of impressive: at the age of 80, only four feet, ten inches tall and one hundred pounds, she could still demonstrate all forty throwing techniques. She even continued teaching judo until she was 98! Her personal motto, "Be strong, be gentle, be beautiful," which correlates to her practice of judo, inspires us to view gentleness as a source of strength.

Dr. Sivaramakrishna Iyer Padmavati

(1917–2020)
Great dame of cardiology

———————

"I never married, but I never felt bad about it either."

Sivaramakrishna Iyer Padmavati was a pioneering cardiologist who, after working with leading doctors internationally, became instrumental to the development of the field of cardiology in India. Tirelessly passionate about her work, she was still pursuing her own research on the eve of her one-hundredth birthday.

Dr. S. I. Padmavati was born in a province of British India (modern-day Myanmar), to an educated family of Indian descent. Her father, a lawyer, was opposed to the idea of marrying his daughters at a young age. Instead, he encouraged their education. Padmavati learned to speak Tamil, English, Hindustani, and Burmese, and following high school, she enrolled at the Rangoon Medical College, from which she graduated in 1941 as the best outgoing student.

After Japan invaded Myanmar in 1942, Padmavati fled to India and in 1946 left for postgraduate studies in the United Kingdom. In 1949, she moved to the US, where she trained at Johns Hopkins Hospital under Dr. Helen Taussig, the founder of pediatric cardiology. In 1952, Padmavati joined Harvard University to study with Dr. Paul Dudley White, the founder of preventive cardiology. When she returned to India, she was offered a teaching position at the women's medical college in Delhi, Lady Hardinge Medical College, where she established the first cardiac clinic of North India in 1954. She worked as director of the Maulana Azad Medical College from 1967 to 1977, founded the All India Heart Foundation (AIHF) in 1962, and became director of the National Heart Institute (NHI) in Delhi in 1981.

Considered India's first woman cardiologist, she received many awards, including some of the highest civilian awards in India (the Padma Bhushan in 1967 and the Padma Vibhushan in 1992).

In 2018, she released her autobiography, *My Life and Medicine*, in which she unabashedly stated: "I never married, but I never felt bad about it either because I am always busy with patients and my research."[29] She was, after all, still seeing patients twelve hours a day at the age of 96, in 2013!

CHAPTER 4

How single women have demonstrated

THE FREEDOM OF SINGLE LIFE

It's important to note that remaining single isn't done only in opposition to marriage. For some women, the freedom of singleness itself is priceless. It's an intentional choice to maintain a certain amount of freedom.

Historically, this freedom in singlehood could translate to different areas of life. Unmarried women might be given more leeway to participate and perform in public allowing them to pursue the life of an artist. Being single also meant having the freedom of their own time compared to the responsibilities of cooking, cleaning, and caring after children and older relatives. This space, agency, and time could be used to be productive, but it could also be used to indulge in leisurely activities.

The women in this chapter help us better understand why single life could appeal to women from different countries and centuries, especially if their wealth, status, or talent, enabled them to make the most of the primary advantage of singleness: freedom.

Without being controlled by a husband, burdened by house chores, or weighted down by rigid social conventions of propriety, single women flourished and thrived as writers and painters.

Because these women left a written trail of their thought processes, we can look back, centuries later, and see some parallels with our modern lives. Even today, for women who value their personal freedom, single life can still provide with certainty what marriage might not: a certain liberty that isn't guaranteed otherwise.

Anna Bijns

(1493–1575)
The Dutch poetess who praised single life

———

Best known for her theological writing, Anna Bijns penned a daring poem in which she encouraged young women to consider how blissful singlehood can be compared to the pains of marriage.

Born to a Dutch-speaking middle-class family in Antwerp (Belgium), Anna Bijns was well educated, which allowed her to write complex poetry and become a schoolteacher.

Starting in 1517, with the growing religious conflict between Martin Luther's Reformation and the Catholic Church, she started writing refrains against the Protestant Reformation. Seeing herself as an "avenging angel of the insulted faith"[30] and encouraged by Franciscan monks, she became a leading voice of the Catholic Counter-Reformation. Her first collection of writings was published in 1528 and reprinted in Latin the following year, increasing her readership throughout Europe.

Even though she was deeply religious and unmarried, Bijns did not join a convent. Rather, she earned a modest living as a teacher and lived on her own. Her decision to remain single could have been influenced by her younger sister's unhappy marriage. Bijns seems to have been critical of the institution of marriage itself, as expressed in her poem "Unyoked Is Best! Happy the Woman without a Man," which praises the benefits of singlehood, such as freedom and independence, while warning of how marriage and gender roles can harm women—themes that are still relevant to a modern audience.

Extract from the poem "Unyoked Is Best! Happy the Woman without a Man" by Anna Bijns

[...]
Maidens and wenches, remember the lesson you're about to hear.
Don't hurtle yourself into marriage far too soon.
The saying goes: "Where's your spouse? Where's your honor?"
But one who earns her board and clothes
Shouldn't scurry to suffer a man's rod. [...]
Her marriage ring will shackle her for life.
If however she stays single [...]
Then she is lord as well as lady. Fantastic, not? [...]

Fine girls turning into loathly hags—
[...] First they marry the guy, luckless dears,
Thinking their love just too hot to cool.
Well, they're sorry and sad within a single year.
Wedlock's burden Is far too heavy.

A single lady has a single income,
But likewise, isn't bothered by another's whims.
And I think: that freedom is worth a lot. [...]
A man oft comes home all drunk and pissed
Just when his wife had worked her fingers to the bone
(So many chores to keep a decent house!),
But if she wants to get in a word or two,
She gets to taste his fist—no more. [...]

To do one's business and no explaining sure is lots of fun!
Go to bed when she list, rise when she list, all as she will,
And no one to comment! Grab tight your independence then.
Freedom is such a blessed thing.
To all girls: though the right Guy might come along:
Unyoked is best! Happy the woman without a man.[31]

Gabrielle Suchon

(1632–1703)
The full potential of single life

————————

"I will describe the happiness of free persons, exempt from such troubles."

Gabrielle Suchon wrote an entire volume on voluntary singleness. Titled *On the Celibate Life Freely Chosen* (1700), it is one of the first-known works to advocate for a third option for women's lives, outside of marriage or religious orders.

Little is known about Gabrielle Suchon's life. Born in an affluent French family, she joined a convent to become a nun, but by 1673, in her early forties, she had renounced her vows and returned to the secular world. In 1693, at the age of 62 and under the pseudonym of G. S. Aristophile, she published her first book, *A Treatise on Morality and Politics: Freedom, Science, and Authority*, in which she defended women's rights.

In 1700, this time as Damoiselle Gabrielle Suchon, which highlighted both her gender and her unmarried status, she published the pioneering *On the Celibate Life Freely Chosen, or Life without Commitment*, one of the first works to offer voluntary celibacy as a third option for women, outside of marriage and religious orders (two institutions that often resulted in the oppression of women by men).

In the introduction to this book, she wrote: "Since women, through the bonds of marriage, are subject to their husbands, attached to their children, and preoccupied by their servants and the pursuit of temporal possessions—prickly thorns indeed that cause inconceivable toil and difficulties—I will describe the happiness of free persons, exempt from such troubles."[32] To support her argument, she referred to ancient Greek and Roman philosophers as well as Christian theologians; she also drew inspiration from unmarried women throughout history, such as the mythological Amazons, the Sibyls of Ancient Greece, and the Vestal Virgins of Ancient Rome.

Viewing secular celibacy as the only true way for some women to achieve their full potential, she coined the term "neutralist" to describe single women who are unattached. This neutrality was meant to emphasize the fact that unmarried women aren't bound, burdened, or subjected to the same responsibilities as women who have committed to marriage or religious life.

Her work was rediscovered in the late twentieth century, and selected writings were translated in English for the first time in *A Woman Who Defends All the Persons of Her Sex* (2010) by Domna C. Stanton and Rebecca M. Wilkin.

Susan B. Anthony

(1820–1906)
The unmatched freedom of single life

————

"I never felt I could give up my life of freedom."

A leader of the women's rights movement in the US, Susan B. Anthony found a certain level of emancipation by living as a single woman, which afforded her more flexibility and independence than marriage.

Susan B. Anthony was born in Massachusetts to progressive parents who supported many causes, including the abolitionist movement and women's education. Having chosen to become a teacher, Anthony immediately noticed she was being paid much less than men for the same work—one of the many inequalities women faced at the time. As she progressed in her career from teacher to headmistress, she became increasingly involved in social reform—until it became her primary focus in the 1850s.

For over fifty years, Anthony dedicated her life to the advancement of women's rights: she collected signatures for petitions, lobbied the legislature, and gave speeches around the country. She was even arrested and fined for illegally voting in 1872, although she refused to pay the fine.

The pitfalls of marriage were one of the reasons she chose to remain single. In 1896, in an interview with Nellie Bly, she shared: "I've been in love a thousand times! [. . .] But [. . .] I never felt I could give up my life of freedom to become a man's housekeeper. When I was young, if a girl married poor, she became a housekeeper and a drudge. If she married wealth, she became a pet and a doll."[33]

She formed a remarkable duo with her friend Elizabeth Cady Stanton. The two women were complementary in many ways: Stanton was married with seven children, while Anthony was unmarried and without children. Stanton wrote the speeches, and Anthony delivered them; Stanton stayed home, and Anthony traveled throughout the states. Together, they launched the newspaper *The Revolution*, founded the National Woman Suffrage Association, and published the book *History of Woman Suffrage*. Although Anthony passed away before women were granted the right to vote, when the Nineteenth Amendment was ratified in 1920, it was named the Susan B. Anthony Amendment in her honor.

Louisa May Alcott

(1832–1888)

"Liberty is a better husband than love."

————

Best known for *Little Women* (1868), Louisa May Alcott was a prolific author with an independent streak. She viewed singlehood through its benefits, especially the personal freedom that it provided her, stating, "Liberty is a better husband."

Louisa May Alcott was the second of four daughters born to the forward-thinking educator Amos Bronson Alcott and his wife, Abigail May, who came from a family of high social standing. Her parents were abolitionists, supporters of the women's rights movement, and important figures of transcendentalism, a nineteenth-century philosophical movement led by Ralph Waldo Emerson. Unfortunately, her father's fantasies led the family to face extreme hardships, which forced Alcott to start working at a young age. While her childhood was marred with uncertainty and chaos, she received an outstanding education that included teachings by the prominent transcendentalists Henry David Thoreau and Emerson themselves.

In her free time, Alcott wrote poetry and short stories. She published her first book, *Flowers Fables*, in 1854, at the age of 22. In 1862, during the Civil War, Alcott joined the nursing effort at the front. However, after six weeks, she became critically ill and had to return home. She wrote *Hospital Sketches* (1863), a realistic portrayal of the traumatic realities on the front, which earned her widespread acclaim. Alcott's best-known work remains nonetheless *Little Women* (1868), a semiautobiographical novel set during the Civil War that centers on four sisters, including Jo March, modeled after the author herself. While Alcott had planned for Jo to remain unmarried (like she was), her publisher insisted on the character getting married at the end of the story. The book became an immediate success and is now considered an American classic.

Fiercely independent, Alcott famously stated that "liberty is a better husband than love to many of us."[34] She never married (although she did adopt and raise her niece Lulu, who was orphaned of her mother) and warned the younger generation of women not to succumb to societal pressure: "One of the trials of woman-kind is the fear of being an old maid. To escape this dreadful doom, young girls rush into matrimony [. . .]; never pausing to remember that the loss of liberty, happiness, and self-respect is poorly repaid by the barren honor of being called 'Mrs.' instead of 'Miss.'"[35] This reminder not to rush into marriage because of the anxiety of being labeled as "undesirable" or "too old" remains relevant today, as that societal pressure still exists.

Ida M. Tarbell

(1857–1944)

The spinster's freedom

"Above all I must be free; and to be free I must be a spinster."

Ida M. Tarbell decided early on that she would never marry, which allowed her to pursue her research and thorough investigative work.

Ida Minerva Tarbell was the daughter of an oilman, and her early years coincided with the oil boom in Pennsylvania. She personally experienced the aftermaths of the Cleveland Massacre of 1872, during which John D. Rockefeller's Standard Oil Company acquired or crushed most of his competition—which included Tarbell's own father. Tarbell's family was profoundly affected by this, and, ironically, Tarbell would later play an important role in the downfall of the oil tycoon who ruined her family.

Tarbell was vehemently opposed to getting married, a decision she made as a teenager. In *All in the Day's Work: An Autobiography* (1939), she recounted her thought process: "I would never marry. It would interfere with my plan; it would fetter my freedom. [. . .] Above all I must be free; and to be free I must be a spinster. When I was fourteen I was praying God on my knees to keep me from marriage. [. . .] By the time I was ready to go to college I had changed my prayer for freedom to a will to freedom."[36] This demonstrates how strongly she felt about maintaining her freedom: she was going to be proactive and safeguard it—including by getting an education and earning her own living.

She enrolled at Allegheny College in 1876 and was the only woman in her class. After graduating with a bachelor's in 1880, she joined the writing staff of *The Chautauquan*, where she published an article defending women's accomplishments, "Women as Inventors." She then moved to Paris in 1891, at the age of 34, as a freelance journalist, writing about past historical figures (such as Madame Roland, Napoléon Bonaparte, and Abraham Lincoln) and interviewing notable public figures such as the scientist Louis Pasteur and the writer Emile Zola.

Her most famous work remains her investigative reports on Rockefeller's monopolies and unethical practices. Originally published as a series of articles, it became *The History of the Standard Oil Company* (1904) and was instrumental in the dissolution of the Standard Oil monopoly by the US Supreme Court in 1911, cementing her legacy as a pioneer of investigative journalism.

Edith Maude Eaton a.k.a. Sui Sin Far

(1865–1914)

The freedom of a broken engagement

"Joy, oh, joy! I'm free once more."

Edith Maude Eaton/Sui Sin Far explored the lives of Chinese people in the context of a dominant (and discriminatory) Anglo-European culture. She also shared her ambivalent feelings toward marriage and her internal struggle between wanting to conform to societal expectations and remaining true to herself.

Edith Maud Eaton was born in England to a white British father and a Chinese mother. Her family emigrated in the 1870s to Canada, where Eaton, the oldest of twelve children, cared for her siblings and started working at a young age to help support her impoverished family.

Between 1888 and 1913, during a time in which anti-Chinese attitudes and legislation (such as the Chinese Exclusion Act of 1882 in the US) were prevalent, Eaton wrote about life in North America from the perspective of Chinese people. Proud of her heritage, she took the pen name Sui Sin Far and is considered the first writer of Chinese descent to publish fiction in North America. Her life and work were rediscovered in 1995 with the biographical study *Sui Sin Far/Edith Maude Eaton: A Literary Biography*, by Annette White-Parks.

In 1909, Sui Sin Far recounted her own experiences with prejudice in *Leaves from the Mental Portfolio of an Eurasian*. She included the story of a half-Chinese woman who gets engaged to a white man, insisting that she accepted to become his wife only because "the world is so cruel and sneering to a single woman—and for no other reason."[37] However, when he suggests that she present herself as Japanese instead of Chinese, the young woman—who refuses to deny her own heritage— breaks off the engagement. Feeling liberated, she writes in her diary: "Joy, oh, joy! I'm free once more. Never again shall I be untrue to my own heart. Never again will I allow any one to 'hound' or 'sneer' me into matrimony."[38] The character shares many resemblances with Sui Sin Far, who navigated a world in which both her ethnicity and her marital status were sources of discrimination and who described herself as a "serious and sober-minded spinster."[39] The conviction with which the young woman rejoices after the broken engagement reflects Sui Sin Far's perspective on the invaluable worth of freedom.

Alma W. Thomas

(1891–1978)
The artist's freedom

───────

Alma W. Thomas was drawn to the arts at a young age. She blossomed into an abstract painter in her senior years, gaining widespread notoriety at the age of 80, and credited being single with allowing her to pursue her artistic whims, saying: "I know I made the right choice. I have remained free."

Alma Woodsey Thomas was born in the southern US, in Georgia, at a time marked by a return of racial segregation laws, especially in former Confederate states, because of Jim Crow laws. To escape racial violence—which had increased throughout the 1890s—and for the children's education, her family moved farther north to Washington, DC.

Thomas, who was born with a hearing and speech impediment, showed a preference for manual and creative subjects rather than academic ones. She was especially interested in architecture but also explored other areas of interest, such as costume design and sculpture, which she studied at Howard University. In 1924, she became the first person to graduate from Howard's Fine Arts Program, and in 1934, she earned a master's degree in art education from Columbia University Teachers College.

For over thirty-five years, Thomas taught art to school children and teenagers. She achieved her prime as an artist after her retirement, once she devoted all of her free time to painting. Because of Thomas's heavy arthritis, which affected her hands, but also with the encouragement of her friend and fellow artist Loïs Mailou Jones, her style evolved from being realistic to being more abstract and expressionist. Drawing inspiration from the nature around her, Thomas became known for her mosaic-like paintings and vivid colors. In 1972, at the age of 80, she was honored with a solo exhibition at the Whitney Museum of American Art in New York City, which granted her nationwide acclaim and recognition.

Thomas remained single, which allowed her the freedom to follow her artistic desires. In an interview with Eleanor Munro for the book *Originals: American Women Artists* (1979), she explained: "I never married, for one thing. That was a place I know I made the right choice [...] So I have remained free. I paint when I feel like it. I didn't have to come home. Or I could come home late and there was nobody to interfere with what I wanted, to stop and discuss what they wanted. It was what I wanted, and no argument. That is what allowed me to develop."[40] This really exemplifies the freedom required by artists to follow inspiration whenever it strikes.

CHAPTER 5

How single women have validated

CRITICISMS OF MARRIAGE AS AN INSTITUTION

In recent years, discussions around the institution of marriage have garnered increased attention. As marriage rates have declined, alarmist rhetorics have intensified, especially among religious and conservative groups who view marriage as a symbol of normativity and virtue. At the same time, in progressive circles, gender inequality in heterosexual marriages has been critically examined, with terms such as "emotional labor" and "mental load" becoming part of mainstream language to address the burdens that come from the unspoken expectations placed on women.

Although these topics ignite impassioned conversations, they aren't just a product of our time. The fearmongering we see around decreasing marriage rates has existed throughout history and influenced public discourse and policy in other time periods. In a similar vein, criticism toward the institution of (heterosexual) marriage has also been discussed in previous literature, by both wives who have experienced it and single women who have observed it.

This chapter focuses on single women who have been especially harsh and direct in their criticism toward marriage (as a heterosexual and patriarchal institution). From their views on the inherent imbalance of power that exists in marriage to their feelings that dealing with an unhappy marriage is more perilous than any of the difficulties that come with singleness, these women thoroughly weighed the pros and cons of marriage and examined the dynamics around them. Unfortunately, they also show that gender roles in heterosexual marriage haven't changed that much—the same concerns still arise, albeit within a modern environment.

Madeleine de Scudéry

(1607–1701)
The tyranny of husbands

"I thank the gods for giving me this inclination against marriage."

Madeleine de Scudéry was a French writer, salon hostess, and proto-feminist who criticized the imbalance of power embedded in the institution of marriage.

Born in France, Madeleine de Scudéry and her older brother Georges were orphaned at a young age and placed under the care of their uncle. At a time when women's schooling was limited, he ensured that both of them received an advanced education. Georges became a successful playwright, and Scudéry first published her writing under her brother's name, to circumvent the limitations placed on women. However, she eventually emerged as a respected writer under her own name.

An advocate for the advancement of women, she wrote *Illustrious Women or Heroic Harangues* (1642), a series of declamations by prominent women from antiquity, such as Cleopatra. She is most remembered for her serial historical romance, *Artamène or the Great Cyrus* (1649–1653), in which she depicted various contemporaries under pseudonyms. Scudéry herself appeared as Sapho—modeled after the Greek poet Sappho—who condemns the institution of marriage by saying "the moment I consider [men] as husbands, I consider them as masters, masters apt to become tyrants, and at that moment, it is impossible not to hate them. I thank the gods for giving me this inclination against marriage."[41]

Like her imagined persona, Scudéry never married. She was opposed not to love but to marriage as an institution. In one of her letters, she wrote: "I do not doubt that her marriage was happy . . . I was less prudent than she was, since three times in my life I favored freedom over wealth, and I do not regret it."[42] For women, rejecting marriage proposals and choosing to remain single could have dire consequences socially and financially. Scudéry avoided the marginalization of single women because of her talent and skills; she supported herself financially with her writing and even won the first prize for eloquence from the Académie Française in 1671. However, she was barred from membership because of her sex. In 1653, she launched her own salon, which became one of the most prominent ones in France. Her legacy was carried on by her protégée, the writer Marie-Jeanne L'Héritier de Villandon (1664–1734), who inherited Scudéry's salon after her death in 1701 and also remained single.

Hannah Griffitts

(1727–1817)
The Quaker poet who wasn't made for marriage

———

"Everyone is not fitted for the single Life,
nor was I ever molded for the wedded one."

Hannah Griffitts grew up immersed in the Quaker ideals of egalitarianism, which influenced her own perception of the world. By acknowledging that neither singlehood nor marital life is a universal fit, she underlined the importance of personal choice and desires.

Hannah Griffitts was born into a prominent Quaker family in Pennsylvania. She was the granddaughter of the politician Isaac Norris and belonged to a network of influential women writers in Philadelphia. Griffitts was one of the most prolific writers of her intellectual circle, but she remained unpublished, by her own choice, preferring to share her work in manuscript form.

During the American Revolutionary War, Griffitts wrote poetry denouncing radicals on both sides and advocating for moderate actions, in line with the Quaker beliefs of peace and pacifism. In 1768, Griffitts composed the poem "The Female Patriots. Address'd to the Daughters of Liberty in America," in which she encouraged women to participate in boycotts to protest the British taxation. Because women were the ones purchasing household goods and since they were able to find alternatives to the products supplied by British merchants (such as making herbal tea from raspberry instead of buying imported tea), they were a powerful force to pressure the British.

Quakers were also proponents of (spiritual) equality between men and women, and some Quaker women—perhaps Griffitts herself—saw marriage as compounding gender inequality. As a single woman, Griffitts devoted her life to her writing and taking care of several female relatives who had also remained unmarried, including her aunt Elizabeth Norris and sister Mary.

In one of her letters, Griffitts wrote: "Everyone is not fitted for the single Life, nor was I ever moulded for the wed[d]ed one."[43] She recognized that single life might not be suitable to everyone while emphasizing how she herself was not made for married life. This statement is remarkably modern in how it reflects the fact that there is no one-path-fits-all in life. It also brings attention to the fact life choices should be guided by individual preferences rather than conformism.

Maria Edgeworth

(1768–1849)

Better single than unhappily married

———

"I am not afraid of being an old maid."

A successful and observant writer, Maria Edgeworth was weary of being trapped in an unhappy marriage. She valued the happiness she found in her life as a single woman and did not want to risk losing it by marrying the wrong man.

Maria Edgeworth was the eldest daughter of a prominent Anglo-Irish politician and writer who fathered twenty-two children. Her childhood was marred by the death of maternal figures: she was only 5 years old when her mother died from childbirth complications and 12 when her stepmother succumbed to tuberculosis. At the age of 14, having finished her schooling, she helped her father manage the estate and also became responsible for the education of her younger half siblings. Emboldened by the experience, she published educational books and defended women's education in *Letters for Literary Ladies* (1795).

Her novels, which received the admiration of her contemporaries Sir Walter Scott and Jane Austen, challenged social conventions, casting a critical eye on how unhappy marriages were influenced by societal pressures, financial problems, or mismatched personalities. Edgeworth herself never married, perhaps because she had noticed too many dysfunctional relationships around her. She wrote: "I have no doubt that my happiness would be much increased by a union with a man suited to me in character [...] but deduct any one of those circumstances and I think I should lose infinitely more than I should gain [...] Therefore, I may well be content with that large portion of happiness which I actually enjoy—I am not afraid of being an old maid."[44] She was happy as a single woman. A bad marriage was a lifelong decision she didn't want to risk.

Although her stereotypical depictions of Black and Jewish characters remain problematic to twenty-first-century readers, Edgeworth expressed progressive ideas for her time: her novel *Belinda* (1801) originally included an interracial romance that culminated in marriage, an official recognition of legitimacy—a storyline so controversial it was removed from later editions. She also acknowledged her own antisemitic prejudice and aimed to redeem herself by writing *Harrington* (1817).

Barbara Hillary

(1931–2019)
Septuagenarian Arctic explorer

———————

"So many people married for a long period of time are boring as bricks."

Barbara Hillary lived a relatively ordinary life until she retired. Unimpressed by the perspective of cruising with "boring" old married couples, she decided to seek adventure by traveling to the arctic.

Barbara Hillary grew up in Harlem, New York. Her father died when she was only 2 years old, and she was raised by a single mother who worked a cleaning job. The family was impoverished, but Hillary's mother always prioritized her children's education. Hillary went on to earn bachelor's and master's degrees and worked as a nurse for fifty-five years.

Once she retired from nursing, Hillary sought out a thrilling pastime. She first considered going on a cruise; however, she realized: "It didn't excite me, being stuck on the ship with married people—oh God think of it—and I can't swim. Unfortunately, so many people that have been married for a long period of time are boring as bricks."[51]

Instead, she traveled to Canada, where she dogsled in Quebec and photographed polar bears in Manitoba. Reading about Matthew Henson, one of the first men (and the first Black man) credited with reaching the North Pole in 1909, she realized that no Black woman had ever achieved that feat. She decided that she would be the one do to so, even though she had reduced lung capacity (because of a previous cancer) and didn't know how to ski. Undeterred, Hillary learned how to ski and raised over $22,000 to fund the trip.

She became the first Black woman to reach the North Pole in 2007, at the age of 75, and the first Black woman to reach the South Pole, in 2011, at the age of 79. Hillary also became a spokesperson for environmental causes and was still traveling at 87, in 2018, when she visited Mongolia. In 2007, she was awarded a special acknowledgment from the Explorers Club.

Hillary's observation that married people tend to get comfortable in their patterns and relationships isn't wrong. She, on the other hand, pushed herself out of her comfort zone, achieving formidable athletic exploits along the way.

Nabawiyya Musa

(1886–1951)
The oppression of marriage

"I believed that marriage was animalistic and degrading to women."

Nabawiyya Musa was an Egyptian feminist and educator who cast an especially severe eye on marriage, viewing it as disenfranchising women. She advocated for women's rights, in opposition to the oppressive standards set by both British colonial authorities and traditional Egyptian society.

Nabawiyya Musa was born in a middle-class family in Egypt. Her father, an officer in the Egyptian army, died before she was born, and her mother was a housewife who was illiterate. After completing primary education in 1903, Musa was expected to marry and remain home rather than study or work. Instead, she became a teacher and never married. She would later write about her negative opinion of marriage: "Perhaps my leaving home at the age of thirteen to go to school was because of my hatred for marriage. [. . .] Since childhood, I had believed that marriage was animalistic and degrading to women and I could not bear it."[45]

In 1907, at the age of 21, Musa became the first Egyptian woman to obtain a baccalaureate. She was also the first Egyptian woman to be appointed as school principal in 1909 and the first woman to be named inspector for the Ministry of Education in 1924—a position she kept until she was fired in 1926 because of her criticism of the British educational system. Viewing education as a key component of women's emancipation, Musa founded two private schools for girls, launched her own magazine, and lectured extensively. She wrote *al-Mar'a wa-l-'amal* (Woman and Work; 1920), in which she argued against the cult of domesticity for the upper classes. She also called for equal opportunities in the workplace to reduce the vulnerability and exploitation (physical, financial, or sexual) of women of all classes.

In May 1923, she attended the International Suffrage Alliance Conference in Rome with her compatriots Huda Sha'arawi and Saiza Nabarawi, two other Egyptian women of Muslim faith. Upon their return to Egypt, Sha'arawi and Nabarawi removed their veils from their faces in front of a crowd, an act of defiance that became a catalyst for the Egyptian feminist movement. Musa, ahead of the curve, had already been unveiling her face in public since 1909, more than a decade earlier. Her efforts to improve women's social and legal status continued until her public presence decreased in the early 1940s.

Nadia Boulanger

(1887–1979)
World-renowned music teacher

Nadia Boulanger belonged to a family of musical prodigies. Paving her way in the male-dominated world of conductors and composers, she advised her female students to carefully consider their choice: marriage or music.

Born in France, Juliette Nadia Boulanger was the daughter of French composer Ernest Boulanger and Russian singer Raïssa Mychetskaya. At the age of 10, she entered the Paris Conservatory, where she was taught by instructors of the highest level, including the eminent composer Gabriel Fauré. She graduated in 1904, at the age of 17, establishing herself as a composer and teacher.

In 1908, Boulanger won the Second Grand Prix at the prestigious Prix de Rome for her cantata, *La Sirène*. Her father had won first place in 1835, and her sister Lili would be the first woman to win the Prix de Rome in 1913. Tragically, Lili Boulanger succumbed to complications of Crohn's disease in 1918, leaving Boulanger devasted over the death of her sister.

Boulanger was also the first woman to conduct the Royal Philharmonic Orchestra of London, the New York Philharmonic, and the Boston Symphony Orchestra. However, she is best remembered for her teaching and especially the salons she held for over fifty years that gathered students and friends to discuss and analyze music. She is widely regarded as one of the most important music teachers of the twentieth century and was even described by American composer Ned Rorem as "the most influential teacher since Socrates."[46] Her notable pupils included the American composers Philip Glass, Quincy Jones, Leonard Bernstein, and Aaron Copland, as well as the British conductor John Eliot Gardiner.

Boulanger was wary of the expectations placed on women. She encouraged her students to either marry or pursue music, but not both, as she believed they were incompatible vocations. She wrote: "From the day when a woman wants to fulfill her true role of mother and spouse, it is impossible for her also to fulfill her role as artist, writer or musician. [. . .] She must give her decision long and careful consideration and weigh in the balance the joys of a family and the joys of a life dedicated to art."[47] While it might seem like an inflexible perspective, it wasn't unjustified given the influence of gender roles. Her student, the American composer Louise Talma (1906–1996), headed her advice and chose to reject marriage in favor of financial self-sufficiency and independence.

Sadie Delany and Bessie Delany

(1889–1999, 1891–1995)
One hundred years of singlehood

Sadie and Bessie Delany were two sisters who experienced decades of transformative US history. At the age of over a hundred, looking back at their lives, they expressed no regret over choosing the path of singleness.

Sadie and Bessie Delany were born to a large, educated, middle-class family of mixed ancestry. After attending university, both chose career paths that benefited society: education and medicine. Sadie was the first Black woman to teach domestic science (nutrition, cooking, canning, sewing, hygiene) at the high school level in New York City, while Bessie, a Doctor of Dental Surgery, became the second Black woman licensed to practice dentistry in New York. She often worked fifteen hours a day and provided free dental exams for public-school children.

The Delany sisters were well established in their community: they became acquainted with many celebrities, including Ed Smalls (the owner of a popular jazz nightclub), James Weldon Johnson (a statesman and poet), William Kelly (the editor of an influential Black newspaper), and entertainers such as Paul Robeson, Cab Calloway, Lena Horne, Ethel Waters, and Duke Ellington.

At the ages of 100 and 102, Sadie and Bessie started working with journalist Amy Hill Hearth on their memoir, *Having Our Say: The Delany Sisters' First 100 Years* (1994), which became a *New York Times* bestseller, adapted as a Broadway play in 1995 and as a movie in 1999. They reminisced about their lives, from growing up under Jim Crow laws, escaping the Ku Klux Klan, and suffering through the Great Depression to witnessing the accomplishments of the Civil Rights Movement.

The Delany sisters opened up about their choice to remain single, with Bessie jokingly stating: "When people ask me how we lived past one hundred, I say, 'Honey, we never had husbands to worry us to death!'"[48] Then adding, "I thought, what does any man really have to offer me? I've already raised half the world, so I don't feel the desire to have babies! And why would I want to give up my freedom and independence to take care of some man? In those days, a man expected you to be in charge of a perfect household, to look after his every need. Honey, I wasn't interested! I wasn't going to be bossed around by some man!"[49] They both had experienced life to its fullest. With a tight-knit family, busy careers, involvement in the community, and enough obstacles to get through, one can see why their interest in marriage was nonexistent.

Yoshiya Nobuko

(1896–1973)
Untying womanhood from heteronormativity

———

Yoshiya Nobuko was a writer of popular shōjo literature. Channeling her own same-sex relationships, as well as her frustrations toward heteronormativity and gender norms, she offered readers new perspectives on womanhood.

Yoshiya Nobuko was born in Japan to an affluent middle-class family. As the youngest child and only daughter, she carried high expectations of respectability and domesticity. Her writing talent was recognized early on, and by the age of 17, she was being published in literary magazines. She was profoundly influenced by Louisa May Alcott's novel *Little Women*, which had been translated into Japanese in 1906. Her parents, however, became worried that her focus on writing would impede marriage prospects.

Yoshiya found notoriety with *Hana Monogatari* (Flower Fables), published from 1916 to 1924 in the girls' magazine *Shōjo gahō*, a series of stories defined by their coming-of-age elements. Yoshiya's writing was inspired by her own life and same-sex experiences, such as "Two Virgins in an Attic" (1920), which drew on one of her romantic relationships with a woman. In her short story "Yellow Rose" (1923), a character decries "the chagrin of parents—for whom marriage represents the sole pinnacle of womanly achievement."[50] There is no doubt that Yoshiya, who defied social conventions by wearing short hair (which was viewed as unfeminine), wrote stories for girls and unmarried women (which was perceived as frivolous), and never entered a heterosexual marriage, expressed through her character her own frustration with society's ideals of womanhood.

Yoshiya would spend most of her life with the same woman, Monma Chiyo, whom she met in 1923. They were together for forty-seven years but faced obstacles because of the nature of their relationship. In order for them to share property and benefit from legal protections, and because gay marriage wasn't legal, Yoshiya adopted her partner. This was the only way to circumvent the limitations placed on same-sex relationships.

Yoshiya became one of the most successful writers in twentieth-century Japan and was a prominent influence in the development of Class S literature. Although she was best known for her stories featuring same-sex relationships, Yoshiya also wrote adult nonfiction and historical novels, for which she received the admiration of the literary establishment.

CHAPTER 6

What single women have taught me about

ADVOCATING FOR ONESELF

In a world in which single women are still often marginalized, this chapter aims to emphasize the importance for women to advocate for themselves.

Consider Margaret Brent, who represented herself in court and demanded the right to vote in 1648. Even though her request was denied—and American women wouldn't be allowed to vote for a couple more centuries—she still tried to earn that right. In colonial America, as a single woman, standing up to the patriarchy so openly would have taken a certain amount of courage.

In Mexico, Sor Juana Inés de la Cruz was not afraid to publicly admonish behaviors she felt were unfair, defending herself and other women from misogynistic attitudes. She might have been a nun, but she was not passive. While she published her writing under her real name, the male church official who recriminated her was, ironically, hiding behind a female pseudonym to do so.

We can also look at Lyda B. Conley and her sisters who defended their parents' burial site through all means necessary—from legal procedures to standing their ground day and night, ready to physically fight against the authorities—and Henriette DeLille, who proudly claimed her Afro-Creole identity, relentlessly pushing through racial and gendered obstacles to achieve her humanitarian goals.

By advocating for themselves first, these women were able to make strides in their own lives while also uplifting others. They did not wait for others to come to their defense—they took charge and faced the battle. We should draw inspiration from them by being more proactive about advocating for ourselves, whether in addressing everyday challenges or tackling systemic barriers.

Margaret Brent

(c. 1601–c. 1671)

Her own legal representative in colonial America

––––––––––

Already regularly exercising her legal rights as a single woman, Margaret Brent dared one day to request the right to vote—over two hundred years before women in the US would be granted that right in 1920.

Margaret Brent was born in England, to a Catholic family that held nobility titles. Because Catholics were persecuted by Protestants in England, she immigrated with some siblings to the colony of Maryland in 1638, at the age of 37. The siblings were granted land from Lord Baltimore, who had founded Maryland in 1634 and established the colony as a safe haven for all Christians, whether Protestant or Catholic.

She remained single her whole life, even though men outnumbered women about six to one in the colonies. This afforded her a certain level of autonomy: as an unmarried woman, she was able to legally own and manage property, which she did with great success.

Brent is known to have represented herself in court to collect her debts and manage her business affairs. Her name appeared 134 times in court records between 1642 and 1650, and she won most of her cases. A respected figure, she was named the executor of the estate of the governor of Maryland when he died in 1647, and in 1648, she was made the attorney-in-fact for Lord Baltimore (who resided in England). This meant she was his legal representative in the colony, which demonstrates just how knowledgeable and trusted she was.

Brent famously asked for the right to vote in the Maryland Assembly (which she would have been granted if she had been a man) on January 21, 1648. She even requested to be able to vote twice, once as herself and once as Lord Baltimore's attorney. Her request was rejected. Nonetheless, because of this, she is one of the earliest-known advocates for women's voting rights in the US.

At one point, because of a shortage of food and money, the colony was being threatened by soldiers who had protected it against a Protestant raid in 1645. Brent disposed of Lord Baltimore's estate to pay the soldiers their dues, which saved the colony. However, because she did this without Lord Baltimore's prior authorization, she drew his ire, and she eventually left Maryland for Virginia, where she lived for the rest of her life. A testament to her legacy, the American Bar Association established in 1991 the annual Margaret Brent award for women lawyers who have opened doors that were historically closed.

Sor Juana Inés de la Cruz

(1648–1695)

A feminist nun in seventeenth-century Mexico

———

"[An] absolute unwillingness to enter into marriage."

Nicknamed the "Tenth Muse" for her achievements in writing and musical composition, Juana Inés de la Cruz chose to become a nun (instead of marrying) because it was the best available option for her at the time.

Born in Mexico, Juana Inés de la Cruz was a very gifted child. She was encouraged to borrow books from her grandfather's library and received some grammar lessons, but she wasn't allowed to further her studies because of her sex.

At the age of 16, she became a lady-in-waiting at the royal court. Her learning and intelligence were tested by men, all of whom she impressed during public debates. Then, at 19, because she had no interest in marrying, she left court. She intended to join a religious order because that lifestyle would allow her the best opportunity to pursue intellectual interests. She wrote: "I took the veil because, although I knew I would find in religious life many things that would be quite opposed to my character [. . .] it would, given my absolute unwillingness to enter into marriage, be the least unfitting and the most decent state I could choose."[52]

Her life in the convent was not as restricted and austere as one could imagine; contact with the outside was not forbidden, and she had access to books as well as musical instruments. She studied theology, science, history, music, and literature; wrote extensively; and even hosted intellectuals in a salon-like setting. Considered the first Mexican feminist, she advocated for women's rights. Several of her pieces were controversial, especially when she questioned, in *Hombres Necios* (Foolish Men; 1689), the hypocrisy of men, by asking who is more to blame between a prostitute and her male client: "She who sins for pay or he who pays to sin?"[53]

In 1690, a high-ranking church official, the Bishop of Puebla, used a female pseudonym to condemn her. She defended herself in her famous *Respuesta* (Response; 1691), however, under immense pressure from the Church, she stopped writing. In 1695, when the plague hit the convent and while she was caring for some of her sisters, she contracted the deadly illness and passed away.

Sarah Moore Grimké

(1792–1873)

Abolitionist and early feminist in the US

"All I ask is, that they will take their feet from off our necks."

Sarah Moore Grimké was born into a rich and powerful family whose wealth was built on the labor of enslaved people. In response to the brutality she saw, she became fervently involved in the abolitionist movement.

Sarah Moore Grimké and her sister Angelina were born in South Carolina to an affluent family who owned a plantation that held hundreds of enslaved people. Repulsed by the cruelty they witnessed, they joined the antislavery and egalitarian community of the Quakers, becoming notable abolitionists in Philadelphia in the mid-1830s.

Grimké also defended women's rights, such as with *Letters on the Equality of the Sexes and the Condition of Women* (1838), in which she wrote: "I ask no favors for my sex. [. . .] All I ask of our brethren is, that they will take their feet from off our necks, and permit us to stand upright."[54] Perhaps these feelings of suffocation are why she never married. She had received a marriage proposal in her late teens (which her brother encouraged her to turn down) and another proposal at the age of 30 from Israel Morris (who had introduced her to the Quaker faith). She refused them both and expressed harsh opinions toward marriage: "O! How many women who have entered the marriage relation in all purity and innocence [. . .] have too soon discovered that they were unpaid housekeepers and nurses, and still worse, chattel persons to be used and abused at the will of a master."[55]

Early trailblazers in the feminist movement, both sisters had already retired from public activism by the time the first women's rights convention took place in Seneca Falls in 1848.

In 1868, the sisters, now in their sixties and seventies, discovered the existence of their mixed-race nephews—Archibald, Francis, and John Grimké—the illegitimate sons of their brother by one of his slaves. The sisters welcomed their nephews, who went on to become successful leaders in the Black community.

In 1870, Grimké—now aged 79—and her sister were elected vice presidents of the Massachusetts Woman Suffrage Association and led a women's march to vote in the local election. Since women did not have the right to vote, their ballots were not counted. Still, the symbolic action inspired many, almost half a century before the Nineteenth Amendment would allow women to vote.

Henriette DeLille

(1812–1862)

Reclaiming her identity and serving the underprivileged

————————

Henriette DeLille was a free woman of color, at a time when slavery was still legal and widely practiced. Reclaiming her Afro-Creole identity, she devoted her life to the underserved minorities in her community: women and children, the poor, and the sick.

Henriette DeLille was born in antebellum New Orleans to a mother of mixed heritage and a white father. Her mother's side, which traced its origins back to West Africa—where DeLille's great-great grandmother had been born in the early 1700s—had been freed from slavery by the 1780s and had established themselves as moderately wealthy property owners. DeLille's parents were not married, as marriage between whites and people with Native or African ancestry had been prohibited in Louisiana since 1724. However, they were in a committed relationship called *plaçage*, a sort of common-law marriage that allowed white men and women of color to form long-term households that were socially accepted even if they were not recognized by the government.

DeLille grew up in this unique situation where her family was respectable and relatively affluent but also suffered from the prejudice of having mixed ancestry. Between the ages of 16 and 18, DeLille might have given birth (out of wedlock) to two children who both died young. At the age of 24, unmarried and rejecting the idea of being a concubine, she chose to focus on charitable work. She was joined by other free women of color, and in 1852 they took private religious vows in front of a supportive priest. Wearing a simple black cotton dress as a uniform, they became known as the sisters of the Holy Family.

They bought property where they educated free people of color as well as enslaved people (which was illegal) and provided care to the orphaned, elderly, poor, and sick. Light-skinned enough to pass as white, DeLille and the other sisters of the Holy Family proudly claimed their identity as Afro-Creoles. This led to them facing opposition from the white community, including resistance from the Church itself, which refused to recognize them as a legitimate religious order until 1876, more than a decade after DeLille's death in 1862 and almost forty years after the sisters had started their work. Nonetheless, after their humanitarian efforts during the yellow fever epidemic in 1853, they received wider public recognition, and DeLille's funeral was reportedly attended by a large crowd, an acknowledgment of her important role within the community.

Cornelia Sorabji

(1866–1954)
Pioneering lawyer in India

———

Cornelia Sorabji faced many obstacles on her path to become a lawyer. Using her expertise and influential connections, she fought to improve the rights of women who were segregated from society.

Cornelia Sorabji was born in India. Her father, Reverend Sorabji Kharsedji, was a Parsi Christian missionary, and her mother, Francina Ford, of Hindu heritage and adopted by a white British couple, was an educator who founded schools for young girls.

Sorabji was the first woman to graduate from the University of Bombay. Because of her gender, she was denied a scholarship to further her studies in England. However, the necessary funds were raised privately by British advocates of women's education, such as Lady Mary Hobhouse and Florence Nightingale. In 1889, Sorabji became the first woman to study law at Oxford University. Her degree wasn't recognized until 1922, and she didn't officially become a barrister until 1923, after women were admitted to the profession. She would be one of the first women to practice law in India.

In 1894, she had returned to India, where she became known for working as a legal adviser to *purdahnashins* (women subject to physical seclusion from men in observance with purdah practices). She advocated for changes through education and campaigned for legal reforms regarding child marriage and the Hindu practice of sati (self-immolation of widows). However, even during her lifetime, her legacy was tarnished by her ambivalent position toward India's independence and her lack of public involvement in the women's suffrage movement (especially given her otherwise groundbreaking work for the rights of the marginalized women in India). In 1929, she retired and settled in London, where she wrote her two memoirs, *India Calling* (1934) and *India Recalled* (1936).

Details around her personal life are sparse; she had an affair with a high court judge who was married and in his sixties while Sorabji was in her early thirties. Aiming to put an end to this, her family sent her away to England for several years, but the relationship lasted until the man's death in 1907. She was later romantically involved with W. R. Gourlay, private secretary to the governor of Bengal, who chose to marry another woman in 1911. Eventually, finding herself opposed to Gourlay in different legal matters, she would write, seemingly referring to her not marrying him: "What an escape I have had."[56]

Lyda B. Conley

(c. 1874–1946)

Battling the system with any and all means

Lyda Conley fought tirelessly for the preservation of her Native American family's burial grounds. From taking legal action to physically guarding the site, sometimes armed with a gun, she used every resource available to her and never gave up, even after facing major setbacks that would have discouraged many others.

Of mixed Indigenous and European heritage, Lyda B. Conley was a member of the Native American Wyandot tribe in the United States. Her parents encouraged their daughters' education, and in 1902, Conley graduated from Kansas City School of Law. She was admitted to the Missouri Bar in 1902 and is recognized as the first Native American woman to become a lawyer in the US.

Conley is most remembered for her lifelong campaign to prevent the sale and destruction of the Wyandot cemetery where her parents and sister were buried. In 1867, Wyandot tribe members had been offered a choice: to either become US citizens or remain part of a recognized tribe by relocating from Kansas to Oklahoma. The Oklahoma-based group then claimed ownership of the land in Kansas and, despite the opposition of (unrecognized) Wyandot individuals who still lived there, began negotiations to sell the land. In 1906, Congress authorized the sale, which meant the bodies would have to be exhumed.

By then, Conley had become a lawyer but still needed time to challenge the sale in court. During this process, the three surviving Conley sisters—Lyda, Helena, and Ida—started guarding the cemetery day and night. They built a shack to sleep in as well as fencing around the cemetery. Signs warned trespassers, and the sisters reportedly patrolled the grounds with their father's old shotgun. Neither Lyda, Helena, nor Ida married; they had no time for a husband or children anyway. Every ounce of their energy went to their fight against larger and more powerful entities such as the Oklahoma Wyandot tribe, the US government, and local authorities.

By 1910, Conley's legal case had reached the US Supreme Court. She represented herself in *Conley v. Ballinger*, becoming the third woman and the first Native American woman to argue a case before the US Supreme Court. Although she lost the case, she gained the public's support, and in 1916, the cemetery received some protection as a historic site—although it wouldn't be until 2017 that it officially became a registered National Historic Landmark.

Sophia Duleep Singh

(1876–1948)
Defiant princess and passionate suffragette

Raised in the UK by two foreign parents, Sophia Alexandrovna Duleep Singh assimilated the culture of aristocratic England but also her father's anger at the effects of imperialism and colonialism on his own family. This complex perspective fostered her interest in social reform.

Born and raised in England, Sophia Alexandrovna Duleep Singh was the daughter of the last maharaja of the Sikh Empire, Duleep Singh, and the granddaughter of the powerful Maharaja Ranjit Singh, nicknamed the "Lion of Punjab." Her father had been deposed from the throne after the second Anglo-Sikh war, in 1849, and had been forcibly exiled to Britian in 1854. There, he maintained a high social status as a foreign prince and a complicated relationship with Queen Victoria, who became godmother to several of his children.

Tragically, Singh lost both her parents by the time she reached adulthood. As a goddaughter to Queen Victoria, she was granted a grace-and-favor residence at Hampton Court Palace, became a fashionable socialite, and participated in typical aristocratic traditions such as the debutante ball. However, because of her racial heritage and delicate political position as the daughter of an overthrown monarch, her social standing was not straightforward. This might have made it difficult to find the right suitor and could be one of the reasons why she never married.

Even if she was completely immersed in the culture of the British ruling class, Singh couldn't ignore the systems and tragedies that affected her family's history. During her second visit to India in 1906–1907, she realized the magnitude of her father's lost empire and was introduced to the growing Indian independence movement. She never became as radical as her sister Bamba Sutherland, who actively supported Indian revolutionaries, but she did advocate for progressive causes; she supported destitute Indian sailors stranded in England and bequeathed equal amounts to three girls' schools with different religious affiliations (one Hindu, one Muslim, and one Sikh), promoting unity.

Singh also joined Emmeline Pankhurst's suffrage movement; she was on the front lines during the brutal assault of suffragettes by the police during the infamous Black Friday in 1910, refused to pay her taxes in order to oppose taxation without representation, and sold the newspaper *The Suffragette* in the street. Her actions were daring, especially for a foreign princess who was financially dependent on the Crown.

Maggie Kuhn

(1905–1995)
Founder of the Gray Panthers

———

"Many people ask why I never married. My glib response is always 'Sheer luck!'"

A lifelong activist who was engaged in the defense of women's rights, health care, and housing throughout the twentieth century, Maggie Kuhn founded the Gray Panthers—an advocacy group that confronted issues affecting seniors—after facing ageist discrimination in her place of employment.

Maggie Kuhn's first job after graduating from college in Ohio in 1926 was with the Young Women's Christian Association (YWCA), whose mission was to educate and support working-class women. Decades before the sexual liberation movement, Kuhn implemented a family-planning class, which was contentious, as some considered it to be an inappropriate subject.

During World War II, Kuhn worked with the United Service Organizations (USO) to coordinate programs (housing, food, childcare, and employment for women) and social events (dances, art classes, welcome gatherings, and religious events) across the US. In 1948 she then joined the Presbyterian Church's social action department, where she fought to desegregate housing, campaigned in favor of a national health program (Medicare), promoted responsible consumerism (urging people not to buy products made under unfair labor conditions), and lobbied for equal salaries for women in the Church. Her work wasn't always well received within the congregation as she pushed the traditional boundaries.

In 1970, she was forced out of her position with the Church because of the mandatory retirement policy, which was set at 65 years old. She decided to form the Gray Panthers, an advocacy group that catered to seniors and whose name was inspired by the Black Panthers. The Gray Panthers fought against ageist laws and stereotypes while also promoting antiwar activism, intergenerational housing, and social protection for the poor. Kuhn's entire life was a demonstration of her commitment to social justice and welfare, a legacy highlighted in the documentary *Maggie Growls* (2003), produced by Barbara Attie and Janet Goldwater.

In part inspired by two unmarried aunts, Kuhn never married. In her autobiography, *No Stone Unturned: The Life and Times of Maggie Kuhn* (1991), she stated: "Many people ask why I never married. My glib response is always 'Sheer luck!' When I look back on my life, I see so many things I could not have done if I had been tied to a husband and children."[57]

Gerty Archimède

(1909–1980)
Guadeloupean lawyer and French legislator

———

Gerty Archimède devoted her life to helping her Guadeloupean community. Because of Guadeloupe's status, first as a French colony and then as an overseas department, her work was transatlantic in nature as it required her to travel back-and-forth across the ocean in order to be able to institute legislative change and to remain involved in current events.

Gerty Archimède was born into a respected family in Guadeloupe. After graduating high school with her baccalaureate in 1931, she worked at the Bank of Guadeloupe while completing her law studies, which she finalized in 1938 at La Sorbonne in Paris. In 1939, she became the first woman to be admitted to the bar of Guadeloupe.

From 1946 to 1951, she served on the French National Assembly, as a representative of Guadeloupe and a member of the Communist Party. She fought so that the people from Guadeloupe could benefit from the same rights that people in metropolitan France enjoyed, especially welfare rights such as social security, retirement, and unemployment benefits.

In 1949, she traveled to the Ivory Coast to offer legal help after the mass arrest by the French government of 150 independence activists led by Félix Houphouët-Boigny (her legislative colleague who would become the first president of the Ivory Coast in 1960). She is reported to have turned down his marriage proposal, preferring to continue her work on behalf of the people of Guadeloupe and care for her family (including helping raise her niece and nephew).

In 1951, she was part of the successful defense of sixteen Martinique workers in a high-profile murder case, which was tried in metropolitan France and, with the background of racial and class tensions, became symbolic of the condemnation of the colonial system.

Returning to Guadeloupe in 1952, she spent the rest of her life fighting on behalf of vulnerable people, often for free. She was especially committed to advocating for the working-class, combating poverty, and increasing literacy rates.

In 1969, when the American activist Angela Davis had her passport seized and was threatened with imprisonment by French authorities while in Guadeloupe (a stopover on her way to return to the US from a trip to Cuba where she had obtained Communist literature), Archimède intervened and negotiated with the authorities to let Davis and her group leave.

Dulcie September

(1935–1988)
Anti-apartheid activist

———

Dulcie September was a South African teacher turned activist who sacrificed everything to fight against the oppressive apartheid regime.

Dulcie September was born in a mixed-race middle-class family in South Africa. She was exposed to injustice at an early age as her own family suffered the consequence of the apartheid, a system of legal and institutional racial segregation that started in 1948.

After earning her diploma in 1955, September began teaching and saw firsthand the effects of the Bantu Education Act (1953), which restricted the education of nonwhite children as a way to maintain existing racial hierarchies. Revolted, she became involved in various organizations, including the militant National Liberation Front (NLF). In 1963, she evaded arrest by hiding compromising documents in her bra, though she was eventually arrested and sentenced to five years in prison. This all happened around the same time as the Rivonia Trial, which would lead to the imprisonment of Nelson Mandela for the next twenty-seven years.

September was released in 1969 with a five-year ban from political activities, teaching, and contact with fellow activists. In 1973, she applied for an exit permit that allowed her to leave South Africa, however, it came with the condition that she could never return. She moved to London, where she joined Nelson Mandela's African National Congress (ANC). In 1983, she was appointed as the representative of the ANC for France, Switzerland, and Luxembourg, and in 1986, she opened an office in Paris, where she was known for her leadership and dedication, which showed in even the smallest details.

On the morning of March 29, 1988, she was shot while entering her office. She was 52 years old. It is widely believed that her assassination was orchestrated by those affiliated with the apartheid regime, as other activists had been targeted through the years.

September never saw Nelson Mandela being released in 1990 or the end of apartheid, but her legacy endures: her memory has been kept alive by her friend the French activist Jacqueline Dérens, her story was told in the 2015 play *Cold Case: Revisiting Dulcie* by the South African actress Denise Newman, and her contributions have been honored through the Dulcie September Annual Lecture, which launched in 2021—a just remembrance for her life's work.

CHAPTER 7

What single women have taught me about

CREATING A SENSE OF COMMUNITY OUTSIDE THE NUCLEAR FAMILY

Women are told, even today, that they will end up all alone if they don't marry and have children. This chapter looks at how single women built their own spiritual, literary, intergenerational, or protective communities. It shows that living alone does not equate to being lonely: single women built connections with their families, with other single women, with neighbors, and with peers. Some even formed intentional sisterhoods, sharing living accommodations and financial responsibilities.

These communities of single women could be part of a larger social and religious movement, such as the beguines, the pious medieval single women who followed a semimonastic way of life. Others were more about personal relationships and the idea of "chosen family."

Historically, single women would have likely been expected to live with relatives, especially male ones. Living alone or with people from outside the family could be considered quite scandalous. Nonetheless, sharing a home with close friends or same-sex partners could be both a pragmatic choice and a desired lifestyle.

Through their variety of living arrangements, single women illustrate that fact that the nuclear family isn't the only familial model and that even by living alone, one can nurture relationships that will provide a sense of belonging.

The Beguines

(thirteenth–sixteenth centuries)
Medieval communities of single women

———

A hallmark of medieval history, the beguines were single women who lived together outside of the traditional patriarchal institutions of convents or matrimony, in communities that offered safety, self-sufficiency, and sorority.

Emerging in Europe during the Middle Ages as part of a spiritual revival, the beguines were pious single women who created informal communities in which they shared lodging, resources, and a semireligious lifestyle. They differed from nuns, as beguines took only temporary vows, retained their own property, and had the freedom to leave if they wished to marry. Additionally, they were not under the authority of the Church, which considered them laywomen. While this allowed them more independence from its authority, it also meant they had no legitimacy in the eyes of the Church, even if they were tolerated.

At a time when many religious orders required a dowry from prospective members, therefore precluding poor women from joining, the beguines welcomed women of all social classes and economic backgrounds, many of whom worked and earned their own living.

For single women who found themselves ostracized or in precarious situations as a result of being widows, spinsters, or even deserted wives, the beguinage movement provided them both autonomy and community; it offered the benefits of communal life (protection and support) without the lifelong commitment required by religious orders.

The beguines grew to become very popular in certain regions of Europe, such as the Netherlands, Belgium, and northern France, with some communities reaching hundreds of members. The largest beguinage that existed, the beguinage of Malines (Belgium), counted over fifteen hundred beguines in the mid-sixteenth century!

As they were living outside of direct male authority (the Church or a husband), the beguines began to be viewed as a societal threat. In the fourteenth century, the Church's opposition to the beguines reached its peak, with official papal decrees condemning their way of life and forced expulsions from some cities. Some beguines were even accused of being heretics, such as the French beguine Marguerite Porete, who was burned at the stake for heresy in 1310. Because of this persecution by the Church, the beguinage movement faltered, and while some communities survived until the twenty-first century, they never regained their momentum.

Anna Maria van Schurman

(1607–1678)

Shared purpose in literary and religious communities

———

Anna Maria van Schurman was an intellectually gifted scholar. The first female university student in the Netherlands, she defended women's right to study and engaged in an effervescent correspondence with other scholars across Europe before withdrawing into an austere religious sect toward the end of her life.

Anna Maria van Schurman was born into a noble and wealthy Dutch and German Protestant family. After her father died when she was around 16, she committed herself to her faith, her studies, and her celibacy.

In 1636, she was invited to write a poem in Latin for the opening of the University of Utrecht (Netherlands) and took the opportunity to lament the exclusion of women from the university. Soon after her public plea, she became the first female university student in the Netherlands. However, she had to sit at the back, behind a partition or curtain, in order not to distract the male students.

Viewing education as a path to become more virtuous, she wrote *Dissertatio* (1641), in which she argued in favor of women's right to study if they had the intellectual aptitude and the means necessary to guarantee that pursuing an education would not interfere with domestic duties. This perspective on gender roles was more conservative—and therefore less controversial—than that of some of her contemporaries; however, Schurman still pushed the boundaries of traditional norms of the time.

Considered the most learned woman of her time and nicknamed the "Star of Utrecht," Schurman was proficient in over ten languages and a key member of the Republic of Letters, an intellectual and international community that included French philosopher and scientist René Descartes, Dutch poet and diplomat Constantijn Huygens, and early feminists such as Queen Christina of Sweden, Birgitte Thott (Denmark), Bathsua Makin (England), Lucrezia Marinella (Italy), and Marie de Gournay (France). This literary community was instrumental in Schurman's ability to exchange and develop her thoughts.

In 1669, despite protests from her social circle, she left everything to join the Labadists, a radical Protestant sect that observed an austere and communal lifestyle. Schurman repudiated her previous work and remained in the community until her death. While shocking, it also demonstrates how important this fervent religious community was to her in her later years.

The Ladies of *Millenium Hall*

(eighteenth century)
The utopian community of single women

———

The eighteenth century saw the notion of female community be reinvented by proto-feminists. In England, a small group of women took it upon themselves to create a refuge for upper-class women who were not interested in the traditional path of marriage.

Published in 1762, *Millenium Hall* was a novel written by Sarah Scott. It featured a utopian community of six upper-class single women who lived together outside of the typical male-dominated household (husband, father, or brother) and devoted their time to philanthropy. Contrary to many writings aimed at single women at the time, *Millenium Hall* wasn't about encouraging domesticity or matrimony. It focused more on the ideas of agency, autonomy, and independence and was inspired by Scott's own circle of friends.

Sarah Scott (1720–1795) was the sister of the well-connected Bluestocking Elizabeth Montagu. She had married, but after only nine months, the unhappy marriage (which had not been consummated) ended when her father and brothers negotiated a settlement with her ex-husband, George Scott. Scott then met Lady Barbara Montagu (c. 1722–1765; no relation to Elizabeth Montagu), who came from an aristocratic family with little money. Suffering from ill health her whole life, Montagu never married and lived on a small annuity.

Montagu and Scott lived together for almost twenty years, from 1748 until Montagu's death in 1765. They surrounded themselves with female friends, including other single women such as the writer Sarah Fielding (1710–1768) as well as Mary Arnold (1733–1807) and Margaret Mary Ravaud (died c. 1800), who lived with Margaret Riggs. Single women living together (without being related) wasn't a common occurrence, as demonstrated by the notoriety of the Ladies of Llangollen, Eleanor Butler (1739–1829) and Sarah Ponsonby (1755–1831), who moved from Ireland to Wales to escape being forced into unwanted marriages. Though their everyday life was quite ordinary, they intrigued, scandalized, and fascinated their contemporaries.

Montagu and Scott dreamed of establishing a real version of Millenium Hall, an "assured asylum"[58] for upper-class unmarried women that would be self-sufficient financially. Although Scott's attempt in 1767, after Montagu's death, was short-lived and unfruitful, it demonstrated the desire for single women (unmarried, widowed, and divorced) to create their own space within a patriarchal system.

Margaretta Forten

(1806–1875)
Intergenerational sisterhood

———

As a teacher and abolitionist, Margaretta Forten fostered connections throughout her community and mentored a rising generation of Black women, demonstrating the valuable and edifying role of educators.

Margaretta Forten was born into a prominent Black family in Philadelphia. Her father, James Forten, a free man, had established a successful sail-making business and was a founding member of the American Anti-Slavery Society.

Like their father, Forten and her sisters were active in the abolitionist movement, inspiring a young John Greenleaf Whittier to write an unpublished poem titled "To the Daughters of James Forten" in their honor. Forten herself was one of the eighteen women to sign the constitution of the Philadelphia Female Anti-Slavery Society (PFASS) in 1833, a racially integrated organization that counted Lucretia Mott and multiple Forten women as founding members. She remained involved in the association until its dissolution in 1870, after the Thirteenth, Fourteenth, and Fifteenth Amendments to the US Constitution were ratified, as the PFASS considered that its objectives had been filled.

As the eldest daughter of her family, Forten learned from her father how to manage business and legal affairs. He trusted her enough to appoint her as one of his executors, which meant that, after his death, she had to negotiate deals and engage in court proceedings to protect her family's interests. Forten was also committed to the advancement of the Black community: as a teacher who taught for over thirty years in Philadelphia, she dedicated herself to improving the quantity and quality of local Black schools, including by opening her own school in 1850.

Since she never married and lived at home, she devoted a lot of time to her family; she helped raise her motherless niece, Charlotte Forten Grimké (1837–1914), who would later become a notable abolitionist, educator, and writer. Forten also nurtured a sisterhood with a younger generation of women outside of her family, some of whom never married, either, such as Louisa Matilda Jacobs (1833–1917), the daughter of the fugitive slave and best-selling author Harriet Jacobs, and Eugenie Webb (1856–1919), whose father was the mixed-race grandson of Aaron Burr. The young women in Forten's circle forged their own accomplishments, but Forten's presence might have influenced their own perspectives on education, social reform, and perhaps even singleness.

Dorothy Irene Height

(1912–2010)
The civil rights activist's family of friends

———

From the Great Depression and through the decades, Dorothy Irene Height campaigned tirelessly to improve the situation of women of color. Empowering others, she found her own strength in her friendships, which she considered as strong as familial bonds.

Born to parents of African American and Native American ancestry, a teenaged Dorothy Irene Height won a four-year scholarship for college in a nationwide debate about the US Constitution. Originally admitted to Barnard College, she was denied enrollment because the school had already reached their quota of two Black students per year. Instead, she went to New York University, where she studied education, psychology, and social work, and found herself immersed in the Harlem Renaissance, a revival of Black American culture known for its thriving artistic, musical, and literary environment.

Height dedicated her whole life to social work, especially to the benefit of women and people of color: during the Great Depression, she was a case worker for the New York City Welfare Department, and from 1937 until her retirement in 1977, she worked for the YWCA. From 1958 to 1998, she also served as the president of the National Council of Negro Women, where she lobbied for the inclusion of Black women in government, promoted voter registration, and advocated for racial justice. She traveled around the world, from Uruguay to Liberia to India, to speak about women's rights and social justice.

A notable civic leader, she was appointed by President John F. Kennedy to the President's Commission on the Status of Women in 1961 and sat close to Martin Luther King Jr. while he delivered his historical "I Have a Dream" speech in 1963. For her devotion to the defense of civil rights, she was awarded the Presidential Medal of Freedom in 1994 and the Congressional Gold Medal in 2004.

Single but far from lonely, Height surrounded herself with a strong support network, including the civil rights leader Mary McLeod Bethune, who mentored her. In the early 1940s, Height moved in with her best friend Yvonne Ray, and after Yvonne's sister died by suicide, they were joined by Yvonne's brother-in-law, Robert Hall. The trio lived together until Yvonne's death in 1978, and Height continued to live with Robert until his death in 2001. The importance of these friendships is detailed in the chapter "a family of friends" of her autobiography *Open Wide the Freedom Gates: A Memoir* (2003).

CHAPTER 8

What we can learn about

SINGLE WOMEN IN POSITIONS OF POWER AS HEADS OF STATE

It is an undeniable fact that, throughout known history, only a small number of women have ruled nations, a result of the patriarchal systems prevalent in most cultures. Even in recent decades, women in positions of power or leadership have still faced mockery or contempt. These negative attitudes are even more pronounced toward women who are single and/or childless, as they further challenge the conventional idea of womanhood.

This chapter is focused on queens, empresses, and other heads of state who were single, of which Elizabeth I is probably the most recognizable name. Known for choosing to remain single, she shaped British and international history during her reign. Others featured in this chapter might have had less of a choice, as the marriage of royal women was a political instrument and keeping princesses unmarried could help limit power struggles and succession wars.

These women, who were in positions of power at the highest level in their nations, left complicated legacies, sometimes infused with violence and scheming. It's nonetheless important to consider that, while not paragons of humanity or progressive icons, they demonstrate the powerful role that single women could play—a role that has too often been denied to women because of their perceived inferiority.

Seondeok

(?–647)
Queen of Silla

———

The Korean queen Seondeok ruled her subjects with benevolence and skillfully navigated the relationships with the adversarial kingdoms that surrounded her realm.

Seondeok was born in Silla, one of the three kingdoms of Korea, which included Silla, Baekje, and Goguryeo. Her father, King Jinpyeong, had no son; therefore, Seondeok inherited the crown. Even though women in Silla enjoyed a higher status than in most places, her ascension to the throne was not received well by all, and two high-ranking officials tried to incite an uprising. This wouldn't be the only (failed) attempt to overthrow her.

In 632, she became the Queen of Silla and the first female monarch to rule in Korea. Her reign lasted from 632 until 647. Wise and benevolent, she was well loved by her subjects because she prioritized their welfare. She succeeded at maintaining diplomatic relations with China, although Emperor Taizong of the Tang dynasty had originally refused to recognize her as a monarch—because of her gender—and openly mocked her status as an unwed woman. When Silla faced a joint attack from the other two kingdoms of Korea, Baekje and Goguryeo, Seondeok gained the support of the Chinese Tang dynasty while maintaining the kingdom's independence. This laid the foundations for the unification of the three kingdoms of Korea under Silla, which would take place after her reign and last from 668 to 935.

A devoted Buddhist, Seondeok commissioned many structures, including an impressive nine-story-tall pagoda for the Hwangnyongsa temple (which was permanently destroyed during an invasion in 1238). She was also responsible for the construction of the Cheomseongdae astronomical observatory, the oldest-surviving observatory in Asia.

After her successful reign, she was succeeded by her cousin Queen Jindeok, who reigned from 647 to 654. A third female monarch, Queen Jinseong, would govern the nation a few centuries later, from 887 to 897. These rare instances further highlight the significance of Seondeok's reign, which was the longest and most impactful of all three queens regnant.

In 2009, Queen Seondeok's story was adapted in South Korea as a television show, *Seonduk yeowang* (the Great Queen Seondeok), which was critically acclaimed and received high ratings.

Kōken

(718–770)
Empress of Japan

The Japanese empress Kōken ruled not only once but twice, returning to the throne as Empress Shōtoku. The scale of her influence is still visible in the surviving artifacts and architecture that she commissioned during her reign.

Born into the Japanese imperial family, Kōken was the only surviving child of Emperor Shōmu and Empress Kōmyō. Since 740, she had been trained by Kibi no Makibi, a renowned Japanese scholar who taught her political science, and in 749, she ascended to the throne after her father's abdication. She was then in her thirties.

Empress Kōken's first reign lasted nine years, from 749 to 758, until she abdicated in favor of a male cousin and became a Buddhist nun. Despite her abdication, she insisted on continuing to be a decision-maker, which strained her relationship with the new governmental power. Tensions escalated when she appointed the Buddhist monk Dōkyō (her alleged lover and a commoner) to a high-ranking position at court. She had reportedly fallen in love with him after he cured her from an illness, and it is said she would have married him had she been allowed to, as a former empress.

Following an unsuccessful rebellion from the opposition, she regained power to the throne and became known as Empress Shōtoku for her second reign, which lasted from 764 until her death in 770. After she passed away, Dōkyō, who aspired to become Shōtoku's successor, was forced into exile.

Like her father, Empress Kōken was a fervent Buddhist. She completed his project of building a temple that would lead all of Japan's Buddhist temples: Tōdai-ji (Eastern Great Temple). With its forty-nine-foot-tall Buddha statue located in the Daibutsuden (Great Buddha Hall), Tōdai-ji represents one of Japan's most famous and influential temples.

During her life, Empress Kōken also helped popularize Buddhism across Japan and financed the Hyakumantō Darani (One Million Pagoda Dharani), a large-scale distribution of a million prayers that were printed on small strips of papers then placed in miniature wooden pagodas (some of which have survived to this day).

After her reign, there would be no other female sovereign until almost a thousand years later, when Empress Meishō (1623–1696)—who never married either—ascended to the throne in 1629.

Sitt al-Mulk

(970–1023)
Fatimid princess and regent

———

Known under her title, which translates to "the Lady of the Kingdom," Sitt al-Mulk was a Muslim princess who managed to position herself as regent, effectively becoming the principal decision-maker of the Fatimid Caliphate.
Sitt al-Mulk was born into the Fatimid dynasty, which ruled along the Mediterranean coast from 909 to 1171. Her father was a Muslim prince, and her mother was an anonymous Byzantine Christian often identified as al-Sayyida al-Aziziyya. Sitt al-Mulk spent most of her life in Cairo (Egypt), which had been conquered in 969 by the Fatimids.

Fatimid women of high status were educated, and, although not involved in politics, they were influential socially and economically. Two of Sitt al-Mulk's aunts, al-Sayyida Rāshida and 'Abda, both died unmarried and immensely wealthy in their nineties in 1050. Knowledgeable and wealthy herself, Sitt al-Mulk flourished into a respected and prominent Fatimid princess. Like her aunts, she never married, possibly to avoid dynastic complications.

Sitt al-Mulk's father ruled from 975 to 996 as Caliph al-Aziz Billah. After his death, Sitt al-Mulk's half brother ascended to the throne at the age of 11 under the name al-Hākim bi-Amr Allāh. His adult reign was filled with terror and cruelty: members of the elite were murdered, other religions were persecuted, and women were forbidden from leaving their homes. Al-Hākim's own wife and son were threatened by him and found refuge under Sitt al-Mulk's protection.

One night in February 1021, al-Hākim disappeared. His bloodstained clothes were retrieved, but his body was never found. It is possible that Sitt al-Mulk was involved in the assassination plot, although scholars are divided on this matter.

When al-Hākim's 16-year-old son was crowned under the name al-Zāhir, Sitt al-Mulk, now in her fifties, became the regent and established herself as de facto ruler.

Over the next few years and until her death, she reversed most of her brother's overzealous decisions: she lifted the restrictions placed on women, allowed wine and music, and returned confiscated land to religious minorities. She also reformed the tax system and fostered diplomatic relations with the neighboring Byzantine empire. With these changes, she helped restore stability and religious tolerance, ensuring her legacy as a powerful Fatimid princess.

Elizabeth I

(1533–1603)

The Golden Age of England

———

The embodiment of the single, strong female monarch, Elizabeth I directly addressed her singleness multiple times through her reign, portraying herself as wedded to the kingdom of England and its people, rather than a king and husband.

Elizabeth I was the daughter of the king of England Henry VIII and his second wife, Anne Boleyn. She became queen at the age of 25, in the midst of a complicated political situation, following the death of her half sister Mary Tudor, known as "Bloody Mary."

Because she was unmarried, Elizabeth was nicknamed the "Virgin Queen"; she was, however, the subject of salacious rumors, especially regarding her relationship with her trusted advisor, Robert Dudley. When Dudley's wife died in suspicious circumstances in 1560, the scandal was immense, as people believed that Dudley himself had orchestrated her death so that he could marry Elizabeth. Because of this controversy, even if Elizabeth had indeed wanted to marry Dudley, it would have been too damaging politically to do so.

Elizabeth never married, despite high expectations for her to do so. Writing that she preferred to be "beggar-woman and single, far rather than Queen and married,"[59] she also reflected on the negative perception toward unmarried women, stating: "There is a strong idea in the world that a woman cannot live unless she is married, or at all events that if she refrains from marriage she does so for some bad reason."[60]

While Elizabeth's exact reasons for remaining unmarried are unknown, she was well aware of the dangers of marriage (and childbirth) for women: her mother, Anne Boleyn, and her stepmother Catherine Howard were beheaded by her father, Henry VIII, and her stepmothers Jane Seymour and Catherine Parr died from childbirth complications. Elizabeth had also witnessed the difficulties other queens regnant faced in their marriages, especially her half sister Mary Tudor, Queen of England, and her cousin Mary Stuart, Queen of Scots, both of whom faced political issues as a result of their contentious marriages.

By comparison to these relatives, Elizabeth herself led a long and successful rule. She became known as one of England's greatest monarchs, and her reign, which lasted forty-four years, is generally considered the "Golden Age" of English history, a time of political stability and cultural flourishing during which William Shakespeare emerged.

Christina of Sweden

(1629–1689)

The bold, queer queen of the Baroque period

———————

Christina of Sweden was a complicated and controversial figure who never quite found her own place in the world. She boldly defied gender norms in every way, from her choice of clothing to her preferred occupations and love interests, never wavering in her decision to live life the way she wanted to.

Christina was only 6 years old when she was named Queen of Sweden in 1632 after the death of her father during the Thirty Years' War (1618–1648), which raged across Europe.

At the time of her birth, she had first been mistakenly thought to be male, which some scholars have speculated was possibly due to an intersex condition. Nonetheless, as the only heir to the throne, she received an extensive education—like that of a prince—and developed a preference for activities viewed as masculine such as horse riding, hunting, and fencing.

When she turned 18, in 1644, Christina finally started governing as queen. However, she refused to marry, stating: "I declare quite definitely that it is impossible for me to marry. Such is my attitude, though the reason I have no intention of disclosing. I have prayed to God to give me the will, but in vain."[61] She remained steadfast in her decision never to marry, despite the pressure from her advisers who considered that, without marriage and without an heir, she threatened the stability and continuity of the royal succession process. This was one of the factors that led Christina to abdicate the throne in 1654, in favor of her cousin and former suitor Charles X Gustav.

A divisive figure, Christina led a bold but controversial life: she cut her hair and wore men's clothes, had rumored affairs with both women and men, fueled political tensions by converting from Protestantism to Catholicism, tried to become queen of Naples through a failed political scheme with France, and was rejected as potential queen of Poland because of her gender. She was also one of the most learned women of her time, an advocate for peace who played a major role in ending the Thirty Years' War in 1648 and later advocated against the persecution of religious minorities. A notable patron of the arts, she was also connected to numerous scholars and intellectuals, including the French philosopher René Descartes.

Over the years, her legacy has been reclaimed by feminists and the LGBTQ+ community as an unapologetic and strong-minded figure who defied conventional norms.

Zeb-un-Nissa

(1638–1702)
Mughal princess and poet

———

As the daughter of the Mughal emperor, Zeb-un-Nissa exercised her agency and privileges within the limits of gender-based constraints. Using her wealth and influence to support poets and calligraphers, she is also remembered for her own poetry.

Zeb-un-Nissa was born into the Mughal dynasty, a Muslim empire that ruled most of India as well as parts of modern Afghanistan, Pakistan, and Bangladesh from around 1526 to 1857. Her grandfather commissioned the Taj Mahal, her father ruled from 1658 to 1707 as the intolerant and tyrannical Emperor Aurangzeb, and her mother was a Safavid princess from one of the most influential dynasties in Iran. Zeb-un-Nissa received a superior education in theology, mathematics, astronomy, literature, and languages (Persian, Arabic, Urdu), and after she memorized the entire Quran at the age of 7, her father celebrated the achievement with an immense feast and a public holiday.

Zeb-un-Nissa had been betrothed to her first cousin, Sulaiman Shikoh, the son of Dara Shikoh, who was her father's older brother. When her father upended the established order and seized the throne, both Dara Shikoh and his son Sulaiman Shikoh perished, leaving Zeb-un-Nissa unmarried and unattached.

She had other suitors—such as Mirza Farukh, the son of the Shah of Iran—but she rejected them and never married. This demonstrates that she had a certain level of agency and that she likely chose to remain unmarried. Her sister Zeenat-un-Nissat, known for her contributions to architecture, also chose not to marry. The sisters' ability to choose contrasted with the situation of their aunt, Jahanara Begum, who, despite being the most economically and politically powerful woman of her time, had not been able to even consider marriage because of the strict adherence—during her father's reign—to the tradition of keeping Mughal princesses unmarried, which aimed to limit potential power struggles.

Zeb-un-Nissa devoted her time to literary pursuits and promoted literary development by funding poets, scholars, and calligraphists. Because her father had a profound dislike for poetry, she wrote in secret under the name Makhfi (the concealed one). When her temperamental father accused her of rebelling against him, she was imprisoned for twenty years, until her death at the age of 64. She is remembered for her significant literary influence and her Persian poetry, which was collected after her death in *Diwan-i-Makhfi* (the Book of the Hidden One).

Mkabayi kaJama

(c. 1750–1843)
Zulu princess, regent, and kingmaker

———————

Mkabayi kaJama was not a king, but she influenced the ascension of several male monarchs, maintaining a political, military, and religious role at the highest level during multiple decades.

Mkabayi kaJama and her twin sister, Mmama kaJama, were born in southern Africa to Zulu Chief Jama kaNdaba. The birth of twins was seen as a bad omen that needed to be rectified with the death of one of the two infants. However, their father could not bear to have his own daughters killed, so he allowed both to live. Breaking the established tradition was a contentious decision, and when the queen died without a legitimate male heir, the Zulu people blamed the 5-year-old twins.

Mkabayi kaJama took it upon herself to find another wife for her father in the hopes that a new union would secure a legitimate male heir. She introduced her father to Mthaniya, whom he married and with whom he had a son, Senzangakhona. After the death of their father in 1781, Mkabayi kaJama became coregent for her half brother until he came of age.

When Senzangakhona died in 1816, his illegitimate firstborn son, Shaka, rose to power, under the guidance of Mkabayi kaJama, his aunt. Shaka revolutionized traditional warfare and led the Zulu from a relatively minor clan to a powerful kingdom. But after his mother's death in 1827, he became erratic and tyrannical: he had people executed and forbade crops from being planted and cows from being milked. Now a threat to the Zulu kingdom, Shaka was assassinated by his half brothers in 1828. According to some versions of the story, this assassination had been plotted by Mkabayi kaJama, who then had all the participants executed for treason, except one of her nephews, Dingane, who became the next Zulu leader.

Mkabayi kaJama never married and had no children, although it's hard to know whether she was following an accepted tradition (as celibacy was not uncommon for women in political or religious roles) or whether it was a personal choice reflecting her rejection of the role of wife and mother. Nonetheless, it is clear that Mkabayi kaJama went beyond the traditional role of women by taking on functions that were the realm of men, such as being, in essence, a kingmaker.

After playing a key role in the rise and installation of multiple kings, Mkabayi kaJama eventually fell out of favor. Because of the nature of oral history, details of her life vary, but there is no question that she exerted considerable—and at times ruthless—influence.

Dame Nita Barrow

(1916–1995)
Governor-general of Barbados

_____

After an illustrious career in nursing and health care administration, Dame Nita Barrow became the first female governor-general of Barbados.

Born on the Caribbean island of Barbados, Nita Barrow belonged to a prominent family. Her younger brother, Errol Barrow, would lead Barbados to independence and became the country's first prime minister in 1966.

Barrow studied nursing at three prestigious institutions: the University of Toronto, the University of Edinburgh, and Columbia University. She worked in nursing and health care administration for many years, both in Barbados and Jamaica, rising to leadership positions such as principal nursing officer of Jamaica in 1956 and public health advisor to the World Health Organization (WHO) in 1964.

Barrow used her platform and expertise to advocate for different causes; she fought against racism and poverty and was an outspoken advocate for adult education, women's rights, and health care. Among many projects, she organized the forum for the 1985 World Conference on Women in Nairobi (Kenya), which welcomed over fifteen thousand people for an intersectional discussion on women's issues—from female genital mutilation to lesbian rights. In developing countries, she defended the value of traditional medicine and healing practices, as they were more accessible to the local population than Western medicine. She traveled to more than eighty countries to promote her advocacy and received worldwide recognition for her achievements: she was appointed as Dame of the Order of St. Andrew's in 1980 and Dame Grand Cross of the Most Distinguished Order of St. Michael and St. George in 1990.

In 1986, Barrow also became the first woman ambassador of Barbados to the United Nations, and she was the only woman to be part of the Commonwealth Eminent Persons Group, which was composed of eight high-level individuals tasked with investigating apartheid in South Africa. She visited the imprisoned Nelson Mandela and advocated for his release.

Barrow then became the first female governor-general of Barbados from 1990 until her death in 1995. Her biography, _Dame Nita: Caribbean Woman, World Citizen_ (1995), was written by her friend and journalist Woodie Blackman, and her leadership strategies were examined in _Stronger, Surer, Bolder: Ruth Nita Barrow_ (2001), edited by Eudine Barriteau and Alan Cobley.

CHAPTER 9

What single women have taught me about

EMBRACING INDIVIDUALITY AND EACH PERSON'S UNIQUE PATH

Even today, choosing to follow a path outside of traditional heteronormative expectations can feel daunting. Yet, by reflecting on the lives of trailblazing single women from history, I'm inspired by the resilience they showed in living life on their own terms. Many of these women navigated a tight line between societal acceptance and marginalization. In the end, despite the challenges they faced, it's their individuality that left an enduring imprint on history.

Take Ma Shouzhen, for instance, a sixteenth-century Chinese courtesan whose artistry and poetry eclipsed the stigma of her profession. Or Jeanne Mance, who eschewed marriage and religious life in France to pursue the unexpected goal of setting up Montréal's first hospital in Canada in the seventeenth century.

Throughout the twentieth century, we find more examples of women who paved their own path while facing discrimination due to their ethnicity, gender, or sexual orientation. Dr. Margaret Chung, the R&B singer Willie Mae Thornton, and the protest singer Colette Magny all rejected societal norms in various ways—through their attire, sexual identities, and the unapologetic pursuit of careers they carved without society's approval.

The women in this chapter are not easily categorizable and their one-of-a-kind life stories are shaped by their refusal to suppress their individuality. Instead, they forged their own paths, leaving society to clutch its pearls in their wake. Quite an empowering way to live!

Ma Shouzhen

(1548–1604)
Remarkable Ming dynasty courtesan

Ma Shouzhen was a Chinese courtesan who enjoyed an elevated social status thanks to her literary and artistic talents: she was a poet and artist whose cultural legacy has eclipsed the stigma typically associated with courtesans.

Although little is known about Ma Shouzhen's early life, we know that she was a courtesan during the Ming dynasty in China and lived in Nanjing, an important cultural and economic city.

Contrary to upper-class women who were physically separated from men, confined to the home's inner quarters, and whose education was limited to matters related to domesticity and virtue, elite courtesans interacted with men in public and were taught music, singing, dancing, calligraphy, poetry, and painting—a versatile set of skills used to entertain officials and learned men.

Ma Shouzhen herself would become one of the most famous courtesans of the Ming dynasty; her talents as a painter, poet, playwright, and performer were well recognized and celebrated.

Her earliest-known painting, a hanging scroll from 1563, was composed when she was 15, and at the age of 18, she created an album of paintings for Peng Nian, a prominent member of literary society. She was especially known for her depictions of orchids, which is why she is often referred to as Ma Xianglan (Orchid of the River Xiang), but she was also a writer who published her first collection of poems in 1591 and wrote a dramatic play, *Sansheng zhuan yuzan ji* (Three Lives and a Jade Hairpin).

As a courtesan, she had multiple patrons, but her most famous relationship was her love affair with the literary Wang Zhideng, whom she knew for over thirty years. She even proposed to him after he came to her help in a difficult situation. Although he refused, they remained in contact their whole lives and Ma organized a lavish birthday celebration for him in 1604. When she passed away from an illness in her fifties, Wang wrote twelve eulogies in her honor, as well as her biography.

Although her legacy isn't well known in Western countries, the work of scholars such as Dr. Ellen Johnston Laing and Dr. Monica Merlin have made her life and work accessible to foreign readers, allowing us to discover her intriguing life and legacy.

Jeanne Mance

(1606–1673)

Hospital administrator and cofounder of Montréal

———

Jeanne Mance's life should have probably been that of a typical *bourgeoise* woman, characterized by the traditional milestones of marriage and motherhood. However, she chose to step outside of conventions and follow an uncommon path, one that took her across the oceans and shaped the world as we know it today.

Jeanne Mance was born in France to a respected bourgeois family. Her father was the king's proctor (a lawyer), and she was educated at the newly established Ursuline convent. After the early death of both her parents, as the second eldest of twelve children, Mance took over the care and education of her many siblings. Throughout the Thirty Years' War—which devastated Europe between 1618 and 1648—and a devastating plague epidemic in the mid-1630s, Mance gained valuable skills by nursing the wounded and the ill.

At a time when a woman had only two options, marriage or religious orders, Mance showed interest in neither. In her mid-thirties, she learned about the possibility of doing missionary work in New France (now Canada). Her unique story as an unmarried woman wanting to travel across the Atlantic for colonial and religious purpose fascinated Paris, and even the queen herself, Anne of Austria, mother of Louis XIV, showed support for Mance's work.

Mance left for New France with the mission of building and managing a hospital, which was financed by Madame de Bullion. The expedition, led by Paul de Chomedey de Maisonneuve, settled and founded Montréal in 1642, and the construction of the Hôtel-Dieu hospital started in 1645. Mance would return to France three times (in 1649, 1658, and 1662), each time raising funds for her life's work.

During the 1640s and 1650s, the colony was attacked by the Iroquois Confederacy as a consequence of the Beaver Wars—a decades-long conflict over the fur trade which lasted until 1701. The French colonists were allied with the Hurons and Algonquins against the Iroquois, but the colony was at risk of being decimated. Mance redirected funds to help recruit soldiers to defend and save the colony.

An influential figure in her community until her death, Mance might have inspired other women to forgo the traditional path of marriage, such as her goddaughter Jeanne Le Ber (1662–1714), who, despite being one of the most eligible women in Montréal, turned down marriage proposals to live as a religious recluse.

Hester Lucy Stanhope

(1776–1839)

North Africa and Middle East explorer

Hester Lucy Stanhope's journey as an explorer was certainly facilitated by her family's wealth and privilege. Nonetheless, she defied many of the social conventions of her time by traveling without a chaperone, wearing male clothing, and never marrying. She disregarded other's concerns about her own life by saying, "Provided I have my own way, the world may have theirs."[62]

Hester Lucy Stanhope was born into a well-connected and wealthy British aristocratic family. Her father was an eccentric scientist, and her maternal uncle was Prime Minister William Pitt the Younger.

In 1810, unmarried and in her mid-thirties, she left England to travel to Gibraltar, Malta, Athens (where she met the famed English author Lord Byron), and Constantinople. After her clothes were lost in a shipwreck, she started wearing male Turkish outfits—a rather outlandish choice at the time. Continuing her travels, she was well received by local leaders in Cairo, Jerusalem, Damascus, and Palmyra. She even led the archaeological expedition to Ashkelon in 1815.

Tall, outspoken, and confident, she was able to defy traditional gender norms and expectations because of her social status, which allowed her unusual freedom.

She was romantically linked to the philanderer Granville Leveson-Gower and to the British adventurer Michael Bruce, twelve years her junior, whom she had met during her travels in 1810. However, she never married or returned to England. Instead, she settled in Lebanon and spent the last few years of her life as a recluse in an abandoned monastery.

Stanhope's story as an unmarried woman embarking on long, arduous journeys is quite unique, as demonstrated by how rarely it happened: a hundred years before Stanhope, Celia Fiennes (1662–1741) explored parts of England on horseback just to experience leisurely travel, and, a hundred years after Stanhope, Gertrude Bell (1868–1926) would become notable for her influence and work in the Middle East alongside T. E. Lawrence ("Lawrence of Arabia"), inspiring the movie *Queen of the Desert* (2015), with Nicole Kidman, and the documentary *Letters from Baghdad* (2016), with Tilda Swinton.

Dr. Margaret Chung

(1889–1959)

Surgeon and World War II celebrity

Not only did Dr. Margaret Chung overcome racial and gender discrimination to become a medical doctor, she defied conventions to live on her own terms: she formed friendships with other marginalized individuals, wore what would typically be considered male attire, went at times by the nickname "Mike," and became a patriotic celebrity who would inspire World War II comic book and movie characters.

Margaret Chung was born to Chinese parents who had immigrated to California in the 1870s. Her mother had arrived as a child and worked as a *mui-tsai* (an unpaid servant girl) until she was helped out of that precarious situation by Presbyterian missionaries. She converted to Christianism and encouraged her daughter's ambition to become a medical missionary in China. Because her parents were impoverished and chronically ill, Chung started working at the age of 10, while still attending school.

In 1916, she graduated with a medical degree from the University of Southern California's College of Physicians and Surgeons, making her the first-known Asian American female physician in the US. After being denied an appointment as a medical missionary in China because of her race (as only white women were accepted by the missionary organization), she worked in Chicago and Los Angeles.

In 1922, Chung settled her Western-style medical practice in San Francisco's Chinatown. Her ethnicity, marital status (as an unmarried woman), speculation about her sexuality (because of her affinity for masculine clothing and her close friendship with the lesbian poet Elsa Gidlow) as well as suspicions about her medical activity (such as referrals for illegal abortions) were all used to try and discredit her qualifications as a doctor.

During the Second Sino-Japanese War (1937–1945) and the Second World War (1939–1945), she recruited pilots for the Flying Tigers, hosted hundreds of aviators, who called her "Mom Chung," and helped establish WAVES, the women's branch of the US Naval Reserve. She was also the inspiration for the character of Dr. Mary Ling in the 1939 film *King of Chinatown*, played by her friend Anna May Wong, and was depicted in the *Real Heroes* comic books in 1943.

Despite her achievements and Hollywood connections, her autobiography was never published, but the first comprehensive biography, *Doctor Mom Chung of the Fair-Haired Bastards*, by Judy Tzu-Chun Wu, was released in 2005.

Greta Garbo

(1905–1990)
The enigmatic and solitary Hollywood icon

———

Greta Garbo took the US by storm during the golden era of silent movies. Achieving the highest recognition and popularity as an actress, she chose to retire from the public view and live in relative solitude, a lifestyle she preferred and was able to pursue thanks to her successful career.

Born in Sweden to blue-collar workers, Greta Garbo grew up in poverty and lost her father in her teen years. Having developed an interest in acting, she studied at the prestigious Dramatens Elevskola (Royal Dramatic Theatre's Acting School) in Stockholm from 1922 to 1924. In 1924, she appeared in the movie *The Saga of Gösta Berling*, which was based on a novel of the same name by the Swedish author and Nobel Prize recipient Selma Lagerlöf. Her performance caught the attention of Louis B. Mayer, cofounder of the Metro-Goldwyn-Mayer (MGM) studio, who invited her to Hollywood.

Garbo arrived in the US in 1925 without speaking a word of English. However, this did not limit her acting roles as silent movies had no spoken dialogue and "talkies" wouldn't become the norm until the 1930s—a transition which she successfully navigated. She quickly established herself as one of Hollywood's greatest actresses: she was especially known for portraying dramatic heroines, such as the fictional Anna Karenina and characters based on the lives of Mata Hari and Queen Christina of Sweden. By the mid-1930s, she was reportedly the highest-paid actor or actress in America.

After making twenty-four movies, she retired from the movie industry in 1941, at the age of 36. Nevertheless, she continued to be a reference point in pop culture, with other women being compared to her such as the lawyer Fanny Holtzmann, who was nicknamed the "Greta Garbo of the bar," the aviator Jean Batten, who was called the "Greta Garbo of the skies," or the artist Marisol, who was referred to as the "Latin Garbo."

Preferring to spend time alone or with close friends, Garbo avoided social functions and even awards ceremonies—which only furthered her enigmatic reputation. She was romantically linked to several prominent men and women. Although two of her admirers, her costar John Gilbert and the Swedish publisher Lars Saxon, are said to have proposed marriage, Garbo never married. When asked about it, she simply answered, "If you are blessed, you are blessed, whether you are married or single."[63]

Willie Mae Thornton

(1926–1984)
Rhythm-and-blues singer and songwriter

———————

Willie Mae Thornton developed her musical talents around African American choir singers and blues singers. Her deep, raw, and vibrant voice was great for the R&B style, which was growing in popularity. With her large stature and preference for masculine clothing, she didn't fit the expectations placed on female singers—but it didn't phase her. She was more interested in living authentically than conforming to gender and social norms.

Willie Mae Thornton was born in Alabama to a devout Christian family: her father was a Baptist minister and her mother sang in the church choir. At 14, she auditioned for and joined Sammy Green's Hot Harlem Review in Atlanta. She taught herself how to play different instruments such as the harmonica and the drums, and mimicked the singing style of blues performers such as Bessie Smith and Memphis Minnie.

In 1948, she moved to Houston, and in 1951, she was signed by Peacock Records (an influential rhythm-and-blues record label). She became famous with the hit song "Hound Dog" in 1952, which reached number 1 on R&B charts in 1953. Although the song had been written specifically for her, her rendition was eclipsed by Elvis Presley's cover in 1956, which became more famous and continues to be the best known version to this day.

In the early 1960s, Thornton wrote and recorded the song "Ball and Chain." It became popular after it was interpreted by Janis Joplin—with Thornton's express permission—in 1968. However, because the copyright belonged to the recording company, Thornton did not receive any royalties from the song.

With the blues revival in the late 1960s, her career picked back up. She performed with Muddy Waters, B. B. King, and Aretha Franklin, toured across the US and Europe, and recorded several albums—finding new opportunities alongside these famed artists.

Her tall and large stature as well as her preference toward wearing what would be considered male clothing were all parts of her distinctive identity. She lived according to her own rules, prioritizing her music and self-expression despite racial discrimination which limited her success and earning opportunities. Her defiance of societal norms and her groundbreaking contributions to music have led to her recognition and celebration in recent years—especially by Black, feminist, and queer communities.

Colette Magny

(1926–1997)
Bisexual protest singer

———————

Colette Magny was living a conventional life when she quit her job in her mid-30s to pursue her aspirations as a singer. Known for her distinct voice and experimental style, she was at times popular or controversial. Her weight and appearance were often a source of criticism, and she became a polarizing figure once she started using her songs to share her political opinions.

Colette Magny was born in Paris and lived a relatively ordinary life until her mid-30s. She worked in the translation department for the Organization for Economic Co-operation and Development (OECD) for almost fifteen years, until she quit her job in 1962, at the age of 36, to pursue singing full-time.

Influenced by American blues performers such as Bessie Smith and Ella Fitzgerald, she performed standard blues songs as well as her own compositions. She was noticed by the television personality Mireille, who invited her to perform on her show in December 1962. Magny then released her first hit, "Melocoton," in 1963 and opened at the Olympia Theatre for French pop icons Claude François and Sylvie Vartan that same year.

Dubbed the "French Ella Fitzgerald" or the "white Ella Fitzgerald" by the French press, she rejected the comparison, which she felt was both limiting and undeserved.

Magny experimented with different styles of singing (singing-talking) and musical composition (free jazz and electroacoustic). While she created songs around poems by Victor Hugo, Arthur Rimbaud, and Rainer Maria Rilke, she is most remembered for being a protest singer.

From the mid-sixties until the nineties, she recorded sixteen albums and wrote songs in support of the Cuban revolution, the Black Panthers, anti–Vietnam War protests, the women's liberation movement, working-class protests in France, and ecology. Her activism led to some of her songs being banned from broadcast by the French government.

Despite her decades-long career, and contrary to her contemporary Léo Ferré, a controversial but renowned French singer who was affiliated with the anarchist movement, Magny remains mostly forgotten today. However, she deserves more recognition for her pioneering music as well as her willingness to defy conventions, including by being open about her bisexuality despite the stigma and marginalization it carried.

Florence King

(1936–2016)

Unconventional author with a contradictory personality

———————

"Now that I had a clear picture of my future, my tepid interest in marriage faded.
I would be a career woman and have affairs, like George Sand."

**Florence King's life could be summarized by the title of her memoir, *Confessions
of a Failed Southern Lady*. Uninterested in marriage and motherhood, she felt
torn between the societal expectations and her own desires. Nonetheless, she
found a way to bridge the gap between the conflicting aspects of her life.**

Although Florence King's mother worked, smoked, and swore incessantly,
her grandmother was more traditional and tried to mold her granddaughter into
a "Southern belle"—a feminine ideal based on the antebellum vision of femininity.
However, King was more interested in masculine clothing and anti-conformist values.

As early as childhood, King realized that she had no interest in motherhood. She
tried but was denied a hysterectomy. Later on, she was able to obtain a contraceptive
diaphragm, but only because she lied that she was about to get married. However,
King wasn't keen on marriage either, stating in her memoir: "Now that I had a clear
picture of my future, my tepid interest in marriage faded. I would be a career woman
and have affairs, like George Sand."[64]

In college, she got engaged to a young man, but she broke the engagement after
just a few months. She was then thrown out of her sorority for expressing a potential
interest in having a lesbian relationship.

After graduating in 1957, she enrolled in a master's program at the University
of Mississippi, where she met a graduate assistant who became her girlfriend. King
abandoned her studies before completion when she realized that she could get
paid to write for pulp magazines—low-quality literature compared to her planned
master's thesis on Berenice, a first-century Jewish queen. Her first story was called "I
Committed Adultery in a Diabetic Coma."

Although the life she lived was unconventional in many ways, King, a walking
contradiction, considered herself politically conservative and expressed little interest
in the feminist or LGBT movements. Still, she fiercely defended her unmarried
status, such as in her article "Staunch Spinsters Give Women a Good Name" for the
Los Angeles Times in 1986.

In her entertaining memoir, *Confessions of a Failed Southern Lady* (1985), King
openly explored the sexism, classism, and paradoxes of her upbringing and life.

CHAPTER 10

The role of single women as

PROTECTORS OF PEOPLE, CULTURE, AND LANGUAGE

Since history has often been written by men, the role of women in safekeeping stories, traditions, and language has often been overshadowed. While there are intriguing ways in which women were able to pass down their cultural heritage— such as through their embroideries or quilts—this chapter focuses on women whose actions, writings, or work was part of a larger, collective effort to protect their people, language, and heritage.

Manuela Cañizares's speech that reportedly emboldened Ecuadorian revolutionaries to seize power, Lozen's involvement in the violent Apache Wars, and Mridula Sarabhai's participation in India's independence movement are all examples of women who undertook patriotic actions, often at their own peril.

However, there are also less grandiose ways in which women have tried to protect their heritage. This can be seen in the archival work done by the Native American anthropologist Gladys Tantaquidgeon or the African American librarian Vivian G. Harsh, who both sought to preserve their culture for future generations. Even Encarnación Pinedo's recipes—which were meant for her nieces and not as a scholarly effort—can be considered a historical resource, as they provide a glimpse into the specific sub-culture of the *Californios*, one that hasn't been well recorded.

Hopefully, this chapter will also help disprove the idea that single women without children do not care about the world after them. Indeed, the women in this chapter, single and childless, devoted their lives to ensuring future generations could know, understand, appreciate, and engage with their heritage.

Without the restriction of needing to care for a husband and children, these women were able to have more agency over their time and, perhaps the most unselfish way to live, they decided to dedicate it to future generations.

Manuela Cañizares

(1769–1814)
Ecuadorian independence heroine

————

Manuela Cañizares is known for her pivotal role in the independence movement in Quito, Ecuador. Her fervent patriotism and willingness to challenge the men who were leading the revolutionary movement is considered to have been a turning point that pushed them to seize power the next day.

Too little is known about the life of Manuela Cañizares, unfortunately. The daughter of Miguel and Isabel Cañizares, she had three siblings and is presumed to have been educated since she knew how to read, write, and do basic mathematics.

Ecuador had been under Spanish rule for over three hundred years when the French Emperor Napoléon Bonaparte invaded Spain and placed his brother Joseph Bonaparte on the throne in 1808. In Ecuador, the Criollos (Latin Americans of Spanish descent) remained loyal to the deposed King Ferdinand VII and rejected Bonaparte's rule.

At the time, Cañizares hosted social and intellectual gatherings in Quito, where the royal court overseeing the region was located. It was in Cañizares's own home that plans to overthrow the French-influenced Spanish authority were made on the night of August 9, 1809, by a group of men that included a certain Rodríguez de Quiroga, who has sometimes been rumored to have been Cañizares's lover.

When the men decided to postpone the revolutionary coup and started leaving her house, Cañizares stood in the way and sternly addressed them: "Cowardly men, born to bondage, what you have fear? There is no time to lose!"[65] Inspired by her patriotism, the men stayed to write the Declaration of Independence and seized power the next day, August 10, which became known as *El Primer Grito de Independencia* (the first cry of independence). Although the Spanish regained control a few weeks later, the spark ignited in Quito led to wars of independence across the Americas, and Ecuador eventually gained its independence in 1822.

Almost a year after the Quito revolt of 1809, an attempt to liberate the imprisoned revolutionaries led to the slaughter of over two hundred civilians and revolutionaries (including Quiroga). Cañizares escaped by hiding in the countryside until her death in 1814, at around 45 years old. In 1829, the Spanish historian Mariano Torrente described her as *mujer fuerte*[66] (strong woman), cementing her legacy in history as a decisive player who pushed forward the fight for independence.

Lozen

(c. 1840–1889)

Chiricahua Apache warrior and medicine woman

From a modern perspective, Lozen's path of non-conformity—both within her tribe and in larger society—makes her a compelling subject; however, her devotion to defending her people against oppression from the US government, trying to ensure the survival and preservation of her tribe's cultural heritage, is also especially significant.

Born into the Chiricahua Apache tribe, a Native American tribe living in the southwestern United States and northern Mexico, Lozen performed well in athletic activities and began riding horses at the age of 7.

Seemingly uninterested in the traditional woman's role as wife and mother, she never married or had children. Instead, she served her people as a healer and a warrior.

In addition to possessing extensive medicinal knowledge, she was also known for her ability to sense the distance and direction enemies were approaching from. Trained by her brother Victorio, who became a war leader and chief, she was said to be his "right hand, strong as a man, braver than most, and cunning in strategy [. . .] a shield to her people."[67]

In the 1870s, the Apache had been driven out of their lands by the US government and forced into the San Carlos Reservation, where they suffered terrible living conditions. In 1877, they decided to escape. Lozen led women and children across the Rio Grande toward Mexico. During that trip, she assisted a woman in childbirth, stole horses, and killed a longhorn with a knife rather than a gun so the enemy wouldn't be alerted to their position.

She fought many battles alongside her brother until his death in 1880, then later helped plan and execute Geronimo's multiple breakouts of Native Americans from the San Carlos Reservation.

During that time, Lozen also met another woman warrior, Dahteste, who spoke English and acted as a mediator. The two women formed a deep friendship. They tried to negotiate peace treaties with the US representatives, unsuccessfully. When Geronimo surrendered in 1886, his followers, whom included Lozen, were taken as prisoners of war. She died of tuberculosis at 49, in 1889, while imprisoned, but her legacy as a defender of her people was not extinguished.

Encarnación Pinedo

(1848–1902)

The preservation of Californio culture through recipes

Encarnación Pinedo's recipes represent a slice of Californio history and demonstrate the unusual ways in which cultural heritage can be preserved. Pinedo specifically wrote her cookbook for her nieces, to ensure they wouldn't forget part of their heritage. Little did she know, her work would still be referenced over one hundred years later.

On her mother's side, Encarnación Pinedo descended from Californios, Hispanic descendants of Spanish settlers in California. Her great-grandfather, Nicolas Berreyesa, had arrived in the San Francisco Bay Area with the Spanish expedition led by Juan Bautista de Anza in 1775. Pinedo's ancestors had been affluent landowners, but the family lost most of their wealth during the US-Mexican War of 1846–1848.

Pinedo's mother, Maria del Carmen, had married an Ecuadoran immigrant, Lorenzo Pinedo. The couple had two daughters who were educated at the Notre Dame Academy in San Jose.

Pinedo lost her father—who died of cholera in 1852—when she was only 4 years old. Later on, she stayed home to take care of her aging widowed mother. When her mother died in 1876, Pinedo was 28 years old and already considered an old maid by the standards of the time. Because she was unmarried and had no other immediate family, she went to live with her sister and her sister's husband, an Anglo-American man named William Fitts.

While living with her sister, Pinedo wrote a cookbook, *El Cocinero Español* (The Spanish Cook; 1898), which she dedicated to her nieces who were growing up at a time when the Anglo-American influence was erasing the culture of the Californios.

With hundreds of recipes, mostly from Mexico and Spain but also from other countries in Europe (such as the French pâté de foie gras), her cookbook represents an invaluable record of culinary history. It also highlights the tension between the Californios and the Anglo-Americans, as she titled the traditional English ham and egg recipe *huevos hipócritas* (hypocritical eggs).

In 2003, over three hundred of her recipes were chosen and translated by the scholar Dan Strehl for an updated cookbook, *Encarnación's Kitchen*, which demonstrates the cultural impact and long-lasting legacy of this recipe book—an unusual kind of history book!

Angelina Weld Grimké

(1880–1958)

Groundbreaking playwright who decried racial violence

Angelina Weld Grimké was a mixed-race poet and playwright whose writing centered around the Black experience in early twentieth century America, including the impact of trauma created by systemic racism. Her writings were essential to the preservation of those experiences at a time when Black literature was often marginalized.

Angelina Weld Grimké was named after her great-aunt, the renowned abolitionist Angelina Grimké Weld (sister of Sarah Grimké). Her paternal grandfather was a slaveowner from a prominent white South Carolina family, and her paternal grandmother was an enslaved woman of mixed ancestry. When the Grimké sisters discovered the existence of their mixed-race nephews after the Civil War, they welcomed them and supported their education. Grimké's father, Archibald Grimké, attended Harvard and became a lawyer. He married Sarah Stanley, a white woman, but they separated during their daughter's childhood.

Grimké was raised by her father and, while he was away as consul in the Dominican Republic during the years 1894–1898, she was taken care of by her aunt, the poet Charlotte Forten Grimké (herself from a prominent Black family and the niece of the educator and activist Margaretta Forten). Well educated, Grimké graduated from what is now Wellesley College in 1902 and started working as a teacher in Washington, DC, while also publishing poetry, short stories, and essays. She is best remembered for her play *Rachel* (1916), in which the central character Rachel, a young girl from a Black family, yearns to become a mother. After discovering that her father and half brother had been lynched ten years earlier and after seeing the 7-year-old boy under her care being chased down and struck with stones by older white children, Rachel rejects marriage (and therefore motherhood) because she cannot bear the idea of having to watch her own child suffer from racial violence. In a way, she views the refusal to bear children—in a highly racialized society—as a way to protect her (unborn) child.

Grimké herself never married or had children, and her play was certainly infused with her own sentiments on what it would mean to be the mother of a Black child in America. Her exploration of what we would call intergenerational trauma had some influence on the next generations of Black writers, including later feminist theorists, contributing to her recognition in the established literary canon.

Betsie ten Boom and Corrie ten Boom

(1885–1944, 1892–1983)
Dutch Resistance heroes

Betsie and Corrie ten Boom were two Dutch sisters who helped save hundreds of people fleeing Nazi persecution during the Second World War, putting their own lives on the line by hiding refugees.

Elisabeth "Betsie" ten Boom and Corrie ten Boom were born in the late nineteenth century into a devout Christian Dutch family who was deeply involved in humanitarian causes.

Both Betsie and Corrie were unmarried and lived at home. Betsie suffered from severe anemia and was told she could not have children, which influenced her decision not to marry. Corrie herself had been in a serious romantic relationship with a young man and expected it to lead to marriage. However, his family disapproved, and he married a wealthier woman instead.

During the 1930s, Corrie, Betsie, and their father fostered seven children from different families while the children's parents were doing missionary work abroad. Active in their religious community, Betsie had been teaching Sunday school classes since she was 17, and Corrie developed innovative church programs for children with intellectual disabilities.

After the Netherlands were invaded by Nazi Germany in 1940, the ten Boom family became involved in the Resistance. Between 1943 and 1944, they regularly sheltered five or six people at a time and saved hundreds of lives. On February 28, 1944, the Gestapo arrested Corrie, Betsie, and their father (who fell ill and died in prison ten days after the arrest). In September 1944, Corrie and Betsie were sent to the Ravensbrück concentration camp, where Betsie died on December 16. She was 59 years old.

Corrie was released just a couple weeks later, on December 28, 1944. She was in her early fifties and traveled the world for the next thirty years, sharing her faith in over sixty countries. She wrote *The Hiding Place* (1971), based on her family's experience during wartime, which became a bestseller and was adapted as a movie in 1975. She was also named Righteous Among the Nations by Israel in 1967, which honors those who risked their lives to save Jewish people during the Holocaust. This recognition was extended to her father and Betsie in 2007.

May Ziadeh

(1886–1941)

Changing her world through literature

May Ziadeh was a multitalented poet who lived in an environment in which various religions, ethnicities, and nationalities interacted. She contributed to the development of the feminist movement in Egypt, bridging the gap between Western and Middle Eastern literature, Christian and Muslim feminism, and French and Arabic languages.

Marie "May" Ziadeh was born into a Lebanese-Palestinian Christian family in the Middle East. She studied in a French Christian convent in Lebanon and around 1908 emigrated with her family to Egypt, where she attended the recently founded university. Her father, an editor in favor of women's education, encouraged her to publish her articles in his journal. She published a successful poetry book written in French called *Fleurs de Rêve* in 1910, under the pseudonym of Isis Copia (inspired by the Egyptian goddess Isis), and also translated Western works into Arabic.

Starting in 1912 and for over twenty years, Ziadeh hosted one of the most famous literary salons in the Arab world, which welcomed intellectuals of all nationalities. An early feminist, she was an advocate for women's education and voting rights. She supported the cultural role of women through her writing, including by publishing biographies—written in Arabic—about her contemporaries, the Egyptian feminists Malak Hifni Nasif (1886–1918) and A'isha Taymur (1840–1902).

Ziadeh was known to be in love with Lebanese American poet and writer Khalil Gibran. They corresponded for nineteen years—until Gibran's death—but never met. Although she was fully devoted to him and refused other suitors, Gibran himself pursued other women.

Between 1930 and 1932, Ziadeh lost both her parents as well as Gibran. She fell into a depression and was committed to a psychiatric hospital by her extended family, who seemingly coveted her wealth. Her friends campaigned for her release, and she was eventually discharged in 1938. However, she never healed from the trauma and passed away in 1941.

Ziadeh's work has often been overshadowed in Western countries; however, it shows how women have taken part in broader social movements—such as feminism—within their own cultural spheres, by incorporating their own identities, ethnicities, and religions into it.

Vivian G. Harsh

(1890–1960)

Preserving and sharing African American literature

_____

Vivan G. Harsh was a librarian who established one of the first and most comprehensive archives of African American literature in the US. Her work was essential to the preservation of Black literature and history, ensuring it would remain accessible to future generations.

Vivian G. Harsh was born into a respected African American family in Bronzeville, south of Chicago. Both her parents were college educated, and her mother was one of the first women graduates of Fisk University.

After high school, Harsh started as a junior clerk with the Chicago Public Library. When she graduated from Simmons College Library School in 1921, she was appointed as a branch librarian. Intelligent and hardworking, she was chosen in 1932 to be the head librarian of the new Hall Library in Bronzeville, the first branch in an African American neighborhood.

Her work as a librarian took place during the Chicago Black Renaissance, a social and cultural movement aligned with New York's Harlem Renaissance, which generally refers to the revival of African American literature and culture in the 1920s and 1930s.

She would serve as the director of the Hall Library from 1932 to 1958, and she was influential in establishing a nationally recognized collection of African American history—one of the first in the country. This was an important step to preserve the writings of Black people from past and present generations, which had often been suppressed or overlooked.

Harsh's work received funding from the wealthy (white) business owner and philanthropist Julius Rosenwald, and contemporary Black authors, such as Langston Hughes, donated original manuscripts to her library, helping the development and enhancement of her ever-growing collection.

Harsh also launched the Book Review and Lecture Forum (BRLF)—an adult education forum to discuss Black history, literature, and current events—that welcomed notable speakers such as authors Hughes, Wright, Zora Neale Hurston, and Gwendolyn Brooks. In her work as a librarian, Harsh interacted with her local community, encouraged literacy and education, nurtured relations with the Black literary intelligentsia, and, perhaps most important of all for us today, her archival work (the Vivian G. Harsh Research Collection) became an invaluable resource for future generations.

Gladys Tantaquidgeon

(1899–2005)
Anthropologist and preserver of
Native American heritage

Gladys Tantaquidgeon was born during a period when US government policies actively sought to suppress Native American culture and traditions. While the elders in her community still retained valuable knowledge, her generation faced the risk of losing this heritage. With an interest in anthropology, she sought to preserve and promote Native American knowledge and culture.

Born in Connecticut, Gladys Tantaquidgeon was a tenth-generation descendant of the famed Mohegan Chief Uncas (1588–1683). At the age of 5, she was chosen to become a medicine woman and trained in herbalism by elder Mohegan women. She became acquainted with the anthropologist Frank Speck when he started visiting the tribe for his research. In 1919, Tantaquidgeon and her friend Molly Dellis Nelson were the first Native Americans to enroll at the University of Pennsylvania, where they studied under Speck's mentorship. Nelson, a Penobscot Native, went on to perform in the US and France in the 1920s–1930s under the stage name Molly Spotted Elk while Tantaquidgeon continued pursuing her interest in anthropology.

In 1934, the Wheeler-Howard Act was enacted, an attempt to correct years of abuse as a result of forced assimilation. Tantaquidgeon was hired by the US Bureau of Indian Affairs to help the South Dakota Yankton Sioux Tribe with the transition.

She also promoted the restoration of previously prohibited cultural practices—such as the Sun dance and the Rain dance—and helped tribes preserve their traditional art skills—such as basket weaving, beadwork, and sewing. Tantaquidgeon also expanded her herbalism knowledge by researching the practices of other tribes. Her best-known book on Indigenous medicine was originally published in 1942 and reprinted in 1995 as *Folk Medicine of the Delaware and Related Algonkian Indians*.

Her preservation of Mohegan documents and records—including births, marriages, and deaths—was instrumental in securing the tribe's federal recognition in 1994.

Through her work and by cofounding the Tantaquidgeon Indian Museum in 1931, she helped safeguard invaluable knowledge for future generations.

Mridula Sarabhai

(1911–1974)

Indian independence activist and feminist

———

Mridula Sarabhai's life was driven by her desire to champion causes she believed would uplift those around her. Actively involved in Gandhi's movement for India's independence, she also tirelessly advocated for women's education. While some of her views and actions sparked controversy, she is remembered for her unwavering dedication to her activism.

Mridula Sarabhai was born into one of the wealthiest industrialist families in India. Her father, Ambalal Sarabhai, held progressive views on women's rights and education, and her aunt, Anasuya Sarabhai—who had been the victim of child marriage and later divorced—was one of the country's pioneering activists for women's rights and workers' rights.

Because her family's involvement in politics, Sarabhai grew up around the two best-known leaders of India's independence movement: Mahatma Gandhi and Jawaharlal Nehru, the future prime minister of India. In 1930, the 19-year-old Sarabhai was a participant in the Salt March, a nonviolent civil disobedience act led by Ghandi. For her actions against British imperialism, she would be imprisoned multiple times between 1930 and 1942.

She defied traditional norms by never marrying, cutting her hair in a short bob, and refusing to wear jewelry. She advocated for women's equality and viewed education as one of the main tools to achieve economic independence. She also fought for the inclusion of women in political decisions and launched two organizations (Jyoti Sangh, in 1934, and Vikas Griha, in 1937) that provided shelter and educational opportunities to women.

For years after the partition of India in 1947, she helped abducted women reunite with their families. However, she faced criticism and was called an abductor herself when she insisted on "rescuing" some women who preferred to stay with their new husbands and children instead of returning as "fallen" women to their families.

In 1953, her friend Sheikh Mohammad Abdullah, the "Lion of Kashmir," was imprisoned. Sarabhai publicly supported him (against Nehru's government). She was jailed for a year in 1958–1959 and placed under house arrest in 1965. Her legacy in India was tainted by her controversial political views in the 1950s–1960s, and it wasn't until the 1990s that a comprehensive biography on her life was published, *Mridula Sarabhai: Rebel with a Cause* (1996), by Dr. Aparna Basu.

NOTES

1. Ruth Mazo Karras, "Sex and the Singlewoman," in *Singlewomen in the European Past, 1250–1800,* ed. Judith M. Bennett and Amy M. Froide (University of Pennsylvania Press, 2013), 131.
2. William Rathbone Greg, *Why Are Women Redundant?* (Trübner and Co., 1869), 5.
3. "Lone Women," *Harper's Bazaar,* 28, no. 27 (1895).
4. "Augustus and Marriage Legislation," California State University, Northridge, www.csun.edu/~hcfll004/AugMarriage.html.
5. Amy M. Froide, "Marital Status as a Category of Difference: Singlewomen and Widows in Early Modern England," in *Singlewomen in the European Past, 1250–1800,* ed. Judith M. Bennett and Amy M. Froide (University of Pennsylvania Press, 1999), 239–40.
6. Thomas Hodgkin, *Vietnam: The Revolutionary Path* (St. Martin's Press, 1981), 22.
7. Michael AB Deakin, *Hypatia of Alexandria: Mathematician and Martyr* (Prometheus Books, 2007), 55.
8. Iman Said Darwish, "Courtly Culture and Gender Poetics: Wallada bint al-Mustakfi and Christine de Pizan" (Master's thesis, The American University in Cairo, 2014), Academia.edu, https://www.academia.edu/36044606/Courtly_Culture_and_Gender_Poetics_Wallada_bint_al_Mustakfi_and_Christine_de_Pizan.
9. Asma Afsaruddin, "Literature, Scholarship, and Piety: Negotiating Gender and Authority in the Medieval Muslim World," *Religion & Literature* 42, no. 1/2 (2010): 120, JSTOR, http://www.jstor.org/stable/23049472.
10. Catherine M. Sama, "'On Canvas and on the Page': Women Shaping Culture in Eighteenth-Century Venice," in *Italy's Eighteenth Century: Gender and Culture in the Age of the Grand Tour,* ed. Paula Findlen, Wendy Wassyng Roworth, and Catherine M. Sama (Stanford University Press, 2009), 138.
11. Mary Astell, *A Serious Proposal to the Ladies, for the Advancement of Their True and Greatest Interest* (R. Wilkin, 1697), Project Gutenberg, https://www.gutenberg.org/files/54984/54984-h/54984-h.htm.
12. Mary Moody Emerson, "Almanacks, January 30, 1807" (unpublished manuscript, c. 1802–1855), quoted in *The "Almanacks" of Mary Moody Emerson: A Scholarly Digital Edition,* ed. Noelle A. Baker and Sandra Harbert Petrulionis, Northeastern University Women Writers Project, https://www.wwp.northeastern.edu/research/projects/manuscripts/emerson/output/emerson.folder03.xhtml.
13. Elleanor Eldridge and Frances H. Whipple, *Memoirs of Elleanor Eldridge,* ed. Joycelyn K. Moody (West Virginia University Press, 2014), 147.
14. Annie Smith Peck, letter to George B. Peck, January 19, 1874, quoted in Hannah Kimberley, *A Woman's Place Is at the Top: A Biography of Annie Smith Peck, Queen of the Climbers* (St. Martin's Press, 2017), 44.
15. Teresa de la Parra, *Influencia de las mujeres en la formación del alma americana* (Fundación Editorial El Perro y la Rana, 2016), https://albaciudad.org/wp-content/uploads/2021/05/influencia_de_las_mujeres_en_la_formacion_del_alma_americana.pdf, translated from Spanish: "dignificación de la mujer por la independencia pecuniaria y el trabajo."
16. George Davis, "A Healing Hand in Harlem," *The New York Times,* April 22, 1979, ProQuest Historical Newspapers, https://search.proquest.com/historical-newspapers/healing-hand-harlem/docview/120893811/se-2.

17. Margaret L. King, "Book-Lined Cells: Women and Humanism in the Early Italian Renaissance," in *Beyond Their Sex: Learned Women of the European Past*, ed. Patricia H. Labalme (New York University Press, 1980), 66.

18. "At One Glance: Mihri Hatun," in *Nightingales and Pleasure Gardens: Turkish Love Poems*, ed. Talat S. Halman and Jayne L. Warner (Syracuse University Press, 2005), 35.

19. Didem Havlioğlu, *Mihri Hatun: Performance, Gender-Bending, and Subversion in Ottoman Intellectual History* (Syracuse University Press, 2017), 95.

20. Florence Nightingale, letter to Madame Mohl, December 13, 1861, quoted in Edward Tyas Cook, *The Life of Florence Nightingale*, vol. 2 (Macmillan, 1914), 14.

21. Nancy Mowll Mathews, *Mary Cassatt: A Life* (Yale University Press, 1998), 149.

22. Umeko Tsuda and Yoshiko Furuki, *The Attic Letters: Ume Tsuda's Correspondence to Her American Mother* (Weatherhill, 1991), 75.

23. Umeko Tsuda and Yoshiko Furuki, *The Attic Letters: Ume Tsuda's Correspondence to Her American Mother* (Weatherhill, 1991), 75.

24. Interview of Marie Marvingt by Gordon Ackerman for *Sports Illustrated*, June 26, 1961, quoted in "Chapter 8: Even Cats," *Marie Marvingt, Fiancée of Danger: First Female Bomber Pilot, World-Class Athlete and Inventor of the Air Ambulance*, by Rosalie Maggio (McFarland, 2019), 111–20.

25. Interview of Marie Marvingt by Georges Gygax for *L'Illustré*, April 24, 1958, quoted in "Chapter 8: Even Cats," *Marie Marvingt, Fiancée of Danger: First Female Bomber Pilot, World-Class Athlete and Inventor of the Air Ambulance*, by Rosalie Maggio (McFarland, 2019), 111–20.

26. Anthony B. Chan, *Perpetually Cool: The Many Lives of Anna May Wong (1905–1961)* (Scarecrow Press, 2003), 97.

27. *Mrs Judo: Be Strong, Be Gentle, Be Beautiful*, directed and produced by Yuriko G. Romer (2012; United States/Japan: Zoetrope Aubry Productions), 07:40.

28. *Mrs Judo: Be Strong, Be Gentle, Be Beautiful*, directed and produced by Yuriko G. Romer (2012; United States/Japan: Zoetrope Aubry Productions), 42:50.

29. N. P. Ullekh, "Dr S Padmavati: India's First & Oldest Woman Heart Specialist," *The Economic Times*, July 1, 2013, https://economictimes.indiatimes.com/dr-s-padmavati-indi-as-first-oldest-woman-heart-specialist/articleshow/20855888.cms.

30. Kristiaan Aercke, "Word as Weapon in a Holy Mission: Anna Bijns," in *Women's Writing from the Low Countries 1200–1875: A Bilingual Anthology*, ed. Lia van Gemert et al. (Amsterdam University Press, 2010), 160.

31. Kristiaan Aercke, "Anna Bijns: Germanic Sappho," in *Women Writers of the Renaissance and Reformation*, ed. Katharina M. Wilson (University of Georgia Press, 1987), 382–83.

32. Gabrielle Suchon, *A Woman Who Defends All the Persons of Her Sex: Selected Philosophical and Moral Writings*, ed. Domna C. Stanton and Rebecca M. Wilkin (University of Chicago Press, 2010), 239.

33. Nellie Bly, "Champion of Her Sex: Miss Susan B. Anthony Tells the Story of Her Remarkable Life to 'Nellie Bly,'" *The World*, February 2, 1896, http://suffrageandthemedia.org/wp-content/uploads/2017/05/BLY-NYWorld2Feb1896p10.jpg.

34. Louisa May Alcott, *Louisa May Alcott: Her Life, Letters, and Journals*, ed. Ednah D. Cheney (Little, Brown, and Company, 1898), 197. Project Gutenberg, https://www.gutenberg.org/files/38049/38049-h/38049-h.htm.

35. Louisa May Alcott, "Happy Women," in *Short Stories*, ed. Candace Ward (Dover, 1996),

36. Ida Tarbell, *All in the Day's Work: An Autobiography* (Macmillan, 1939), 36.

37. Annette White-Parks, *Sui Sin Far / Edith Maude Eaton: A Literary Biography* (University of Illinois Press, 1995), 39.

38. Annette White-Parks, *Sui Sin Far / Edith Maude Eaton: A Literary Biography* (University of Illinois Press, 1995), 39.

39. Annette White-Parks, *Sui Sin Far / Edith Maude Eaton: A Literary Biography* (University of Illinois Press, 1995), 40.

40. Eleanor Munro, "Alma W. Thomas," in *Originals: American Women Artists* (Simon & Schuster, 1979), 195–96.

41. Madeleine de Scudéry, *The Story of Sapho*, ed. and trans. Karen Newman (University of Chicago Press, 2003), 20.

42. Madeleine de Scudéry, letter to the Abbé Boisot, December 18, 1691, quoted in *Mademoiselle de Scudéry: sa vie et sa correspondance*, ed. Edmé-Jacques-Benoît Rathery and Boutron (Léon Techener, 1873), 330.

43. Hannah Griffitts, letter to Milcah Martha Moore, n.d., quoted in *Milcah Martha Moore's Book: A Commonplace Book from Revolutionary America*, ed. Catherine La Courreye Blecki and Karin A. Wulf (Pennsylvania State University Press, 2007), 12.

44. Marilyn Butler, *Maria Edgeworth: A Literary Biography (Oxford University* Press, 1972), 187.

45. Margot Badran, *Feminists, Islam, and Nation: Gender and the Making of Modern Egypt* (Princeton University Press, 1995), 44–45.

46. Ned Rorem, "The Composer and the Music Teacher," *The New York Times*, May 23, 1982, https://www.nytimes.com/1982/05/23/books/the-composer-and-the-music-teacher.html.

47. Léonie Rosenstiel, *Nadia Boulanger: A Life in Music* (W. W. Norton, 1982), 101.

48. Sarah L. Delany, A. Elizabeth Delany, and Amy Hill Hearth, *Having Our Say: The Delany Sisters' First 100 Years* (Dell, 1994), 23–24.

49. Sarah L. Delany, A. Elizabeth Delany, and Amy Hill Hearth, *Having Our Say: The Delany Sisters' First 100 Years* (Dell, 1994), 158.

50. Nobuko Yoshiya, *Yellow Rose*, trans. Sarah Frederick, 2nd ed. (Expanded Editions, 2016), 10.

51. Shelby Knapp, "Barbara Hillary: Our Favorite Boundary Breaker," *REI Blog,* March 3, 2017, Internet Archive, https://web.archive.org/web/20230610111830/https://www.rei.com/blog/snowsports/barbara-hillary-favorite-boundary-breaker.

52. Juana Inés de la Cruz, letter to Sor Filotea, 1691, quoted in *Colonial Spanish America: A Documentary History*, eds. Kenneth Mills, William B. Taylor, and Sandra Lauderdale Graham (Rowman & Littlefield, 2002), 210.

53. Juana Inés de la Cruz, "You Foolish Men," *Poets.org*, Academy of American Poets, https://poets.org/poem/you-foolish-men.

54. Sarah Grimké, *Letters on the Equality of the Sexes and the Condition of Women* (Isaac Knapp, 1838), Project Gutenberg, https://www.gutenberg.org/cache/epub/69485/pg69485-images.html.

55. Elizabeth Ann Bartlett, "Sarah Grimké," in *Liberty, Equality, Sorority: The Origins and Interpretation of American Feminist Thought: Frances Wright, Sarah Grimké, and Margaret Fuller* (Carlson Publishing, 1994), 72.

56. Richard Sorabji, *Opening Doors: The Untold Story of Cornelia Sorabji, Reformer, Lawyer, and Champion of Women's Rights in India* (I. B. Tauris, 2010), 102.

57. Maggie Kuhn, Christina Long, and Laura Quinn, *No Stone Unturned: The Life and Times of Maggie Kuhn* (Ballantine Books, 1991), 71.

58. Sarah Scott, *A Description of Millenium Hall and the Country Adjacent* (1762), Project Gutenberg, https://www.gutenberg.org/files/26050/26050-h/26050-h.htm.

59. Elizabeth I, letter to an imperial envoy, ca. 1563, quoted in John Ernest Neale, *Queen Elizabeth* (Penguin, 1971), 143.

60. Tracy Borman, *Elizabeth's Women: Friends, Rivals, and Foes Who Shaped the Virgin Queen* (Bantam, 2009), 215.
61. Curt Weibull, *Christina of Sweden* (Bonnier, 1966), 28.
62. Lady Hester Stanhope, letter to Francis James Jackson, c. 1801–1802, quoted in Frank Hamel, *The Life and Letters of Lady Hester Stanhope* (Cassell and Company, 1913), 27.
63. John Bainbridge, *Garbo* (Doubleday, 1955), 202.
64. Florence King, *Confessions of a Failed Southern Lady* (St. Martin's Press, 1985), 125.
65. "First Cry of Independence," posted August 6, 2014, by the Consulado del Ecuador en Caracas, YouTube, 0:00:41, https://www.youtube.com/watch?v=SVuBmBH7kTg.
66. Mariano Torrente, *Historia de la revolución hispano-americana* (Leon Amarita, 1829), 41.
67. Mike Leach and Buddy Levy, "Woman Warrior: Lozen," in Geronimo: *Leadership Strategies of an American Warrior* (Gallery Books, 2014), 78.

BIBLIOGRAPHY

Chapter 1: Defying Traditional Gender Norms Throughout Ancient History

Gārgī Vāchaknavī

Black, Brian. "Gargi: The Debating Tactics of a Female Philosopher." In *The Character of the Self in Ancient India: Priests, Kings, and Women in the Early Upanisads*, 150–55. State University of New York Press, 2007.

Das, Rituparna. "Mystics." In *Daily Life of Women: An Encyclopedia from Ancient Times to the Present*, vol. 1, edited by Colleen Boyett, H. Micheal Tarver, and Mildred Diane Gleason, 139, 148, and 151. Greenwood, 2020.

Findly, Ellison Banks. "Gargi at the King's Court: Women and Philosophic Innovation in Ancient India." In *Women, Religion, and Social Change*, edited by Yvonne Yazbeck Haddad and Ellison Banks Findly, 37–58. State University of New York Press, 1985.

Lady Triêu

Churchman, Catherine. *The People between the Rivers: The Rise and Fall of a Bronze Drum Culture, 200–750 CE,* 126 and 137. Rowman & Littlefield, 2016.

Hodgkin, Thomas. *Vietnam: The Revolutionary Path*, 22. St. Martin's Press, 1981.

Lockard, Craig A. *Societies, Networks, and Transitions: A Global History*, 4th ed., 124. Cengage, 2020.

Taylor, Keith Weller. *The Birth of Vietnam*, 90–91. University of California Press, 1983.

Turner, Karen. "Trinh Trieu Thi." In *The Oxford Encyclopedia of Women in World History*, vol. 1, edited by Bonnie G. Smith, 248. Oxford University Press, 2008.

Hypatia

Deakin, Michael AB. *Hypatia of Alexandria: Mathematician and Martyr*. Prometheus Books, 2007.

Song Ruoshen and Song Ruozhao

Jia, Jinhua. "Song Ruozhao." Translated by Laura Long. In *Biographical Dictionary of Chinese Women, Tang Through Ming 618–1644*, vol. 2, edited by Lily Xiao Hong Lee and Sue Wiles, 374–75. Routledge, 2015.

Jia, Jinhua, and Lily Xiao Hong Lee. "Song Ruoxin." Translated by Laura Long. In *Biographical Dictionary of Chinese Women, Tang Through Ming 618–1644*, vol. 2, edited by Lily Xiao Hong Lee and Sue Wiles, 372–73. Routledge, 2015.

Pang-White, Ann A. "The Tang Women: The Song Sisters and the Analects for Women (Nü luny): ?–820/825 CE." In *The Confucian Four Books for Women: A New Translation of the Nü Sishu and the Commentary of Wang Xiang*, 71–120. Oxford University Press, 2018.

Robertson, Maureen. "Voicing the Feminine: Constructions of the Gendered Subject in Lyric Poetry by Women of Medieval and Late Imperial China." *Late Imperial China* 13, no. 1 (1992): 78. https://dx.doi.org/10.1353/late.1992.0006.

Shi, Mulin. "Song Sisters, Poets and Beauties, Tang Dynasty." Translated by Xu Kaichang. In *Notable Women of China: Shang Dynasty to the Early Twentieth Century*, by Barbara Bennett Peterson, 223–25. M. E. Sharpe, 2000.

Wang, Robin. "The Analects for Women (Nü lunyu): Song Ruoxin and Song Ruozhao." In *Images of Women in Chinese Thought and Culture: Writings from the Pre-Qin Period to the Song Dynasty*, 327–40. Hackett, 2003.

Wallada bint al-Mustakfi

Afsaruddin, Asma. "Literature, Scholarship, and Piety: Negotiating Gender and Authority in the Medieval Muslim World." *Religion & Literature* 42, no. 1/2 (2010): 111–31. http://www.jstor.org/stable/23049472.

Darwish, Iman Said. "Courtly Culture and Gender Poetics: Wallada bint al-Mustakfi and Christine de Pizan." Master's thesis, The American University in Cairo, 2014. Academia.edu. https://www.academia.edu/36044606/Courtly_Culture_and_Gender_Poetics_Wallada_bint_al_Mustakfi_and_Christine_de_Pizan.

Dodds, Jerrilynn. "Thieves of Pleasure: A Vicious Fraternal War Rewards Alfonso VI with the Artistic and Poetic Treasures of al-Andalus." *Humanities* 30, no. 2 (2009). National Endowment for the Humanities. https://www.neh.gov/humanities/2009/marchapril/feature/thieves-pleasure.

Meisami, Julie Scott, and Paul Starkey, eds. "Wallada Bint al-Mustakfi." In *Encyclopedia of Arabic Literature*, vol. 2, 803–4. Routledge, 1999.

Najjaj, April L. "Feminisms and the Hijāb: Not Mutually Exclusive." *Social Sciences* 6, no. 3 (2017): 80. http://dx.doi.org/10.3390/socsci6030080.

Shamsie, Kamila. "Librarians, Rebels, Property Owners, Slaves: Women in al-Andalus." *Journal of Postcolonial Writing* 52, no. 2 (2016): 178–88. doi:10.1080/17449855.2016.1164968.

Uhl, Patrice. "Wallada: Une 'Trobairitz' d'al-Andalus." *Travaux & Documents*, Université de La Réunion, Faculté des Lettres et des Sciences Humaines, 2000, 21–38. HAL Archives. https://hal.univ-reunion.fr/hal-02158331.

Hildegard of Bingen

Flanagan, Sabina. *Hildegard of Bingen: A Visionary Life*. Routledge, 1989.

Maddocks, Fiona. *Hildegard of Bingen*. Image, 2003.

Chapter 2: The Importance of Financial Independence

Rosalba Carriera

Palmer, Allison Lee. "Carriera, Rosalba (1675–1757)." In *Historical Dictionary of Neoclassical Art and Architecture*, 2nd ed., 66–67. Rowman & Littlefield, 2020.

"Powder and Patches." *The Saint Paul's Magazine*, 13 (July–December 1873): 180–91. Google Books. https://books.google.fr/books?id=V69HAQAAMAAJ&pg=PA180.

Sama, Catherine M. "'On Canvas and on the Page': Women Shaping Culture in Eighteenth-Century Venice." In *Italy's Eighteenth Century: Gender and Culture in the Age of the Grand Tour*, edited by Paula Findlen, Wendy Wassyng Roworth, and Catherine M. Sama, 138. Stanford University Press, 2009.

Slatkin, Wendy. "Rosalba Carriera (1675–1752)." In *Voices of Women Artists*, 12–20. Prentice Hall, 1993.

Lady Elizabeth Hastings

Astell, Mary. *A Serious Proposal to the Ladies, for the Advancement of Their True and Greatest Interest*. R. Wilkin, 1697. Project Gutenberg. https://www.gutenberg.org/files/54984/54984-h/54984-h.htm.

Hays, Mary. "Lady Elizabeth Hastings." In *Female Biography: or, Memoirs of Illustrious and Celebrated Women of All Ages and Countries. Alphabetically Arranged*, vol. 2, 408–13. Fry and Kammerer, 1807.

Hill, Bridget. *Women Alone: Spinsters in England, 1660–1850*, 8, 133, and 174–75. Yale University Press, 2001.

"Lady Elizabeth Hastings Charities." https://www.ladyelizabethhastingscharities.co.uk.

Laurence, Anne. "Lady Betty Hastings, Her Half-Sisters, and the South Sea Bubble: Family Fortunes and Strategies." *Women's History Review* 15, no. 4 (2006): 533–40. https://doi.org/10.1080/09612020500530539.

Perry, Ruth. "Mary Astell and Enlightenment." In *Women, Gender and Enlightenment*, edited by Sarah Knott and Barbara Taylor, 357–70. Palgrave Macmillan, 2005.

Mary Moody Emerson

Baker, Noelle A., and Sandra Harbert Petrulionis. "Mary Moody Emerson Was a Scholar, a Thinker, and an Inspiration." *Humanities* 38, no. 1 (Winter 2017). National Endowment for the Humanities. https://www.neh.gov/humanities/2017/winter/feature/mary-moody-emerson-was-scholar-thinker-and-inspiration-all-who-knew-her.

———. *The "Almanacks" of Mary Moody Emerson: A Scholarly Digital Edition*. Northeastern University Women Writers Project. https://www.wwp.northeastern.edu/research/projects/manuscripts/emerson/output/emerson.folder03.xhtml.

Barish, Evelyn. "Chapter 2: Aunt." In *Emerson: The Roots of Prophecy*, 36–53. Princeton University Press, 2016.

Battiste, Janice. "A Good Aunt Is More to a Poet Than a Patron: Mary Moody Emerson, a Model for Self-Reliance." *WILLA* 5 (1996): 6–10. https://scholar.lib.vt.edu/ejournals/old-WILLA/fall96/battiste.html.

Cole, Phyllis. *Mary Moody Emerson and the Origins of Transcendentalism: A Family History.* Oxford University Press, 2002.

Emerson, Ralph Waldo. "Mary Moody Emerson." *The Atlantic*, December 1883. https://www.theatlantic.com/magazine/archive/1883/12/mary-moody-emerson/539490/.

Elleanor Eldridge

Brody, Jennifer D., and Sharon P. Holland. "An/other Case of New England Underwriting: Negotiating Race and Property in Memoirs of Elleanor Eldridge." In *Crossing Waters, Crossing Worlds: The African Diaspora in Indian Country*, edited by Tiya Miles and Sharon Patricia Holland, 31–56. Duke University Press, 2006.

Eldridge, Elleanor, and Frances H. Whipple. *Memoirs of Elleanor Eldridge*, edited by Joycelyn K. Moody. West Virginia University Press, 2014.

Gautier, Amina. "African American Women's Writings in the Woman's Building Library." *Libraries & Culture* 41, no. 1 (2006): 55–81. http://www.jstor.org/stable/25541970.

Hansen, Rebecca. "'No Man Ever Would Have Been Treated So': Elleanor Eldridge." *Rhode Island Historical Society*, March 22, 2017. https://www.rihs.org/elleanor-eldridge/.

Smith, Jessie Carney. "Elleanor Eldridge (1785–1865?)." In *Encyclopedia of African American Business*, edited by Jessie Carney Smith, Millicent Lownes Jackson, and Linda T. Wynn, 268–70. Greenwood Press, 2006.

Annie Smith Peck

Brooklyn Museum. "Annie Smith Peck." https://www.brooklynmuseum.org/eascfa/dinner_party/heritage_floor/annie_smith_peck.

Engel, Claire-Elaine. "Early Ladies Climbers." *Alpine Journal*, 1943, 56–59. https://www.alpinejournal.org.uk/Contents/Contents_1943_files/AJ54%201943%2051-59%20Engel%20Lady%20Climbers.pdf.

Kimberley, Hannah. *A Woman's Place Is at the Top: A Biography of Annie Smith Peck, Queen of the Climbers.* St. Martin's Press, 2017.

Teresa de la Parra

Acker, Bertie. "'Ifigenia': Teresa de la Parra's Social Protest." *Letras Femeninas* 14, no. 1/2 (1988): 73–79. JSTOR. http://www.jstor.org/stable/23022145.

De la Parra, Teresa. *Influencia de las Mujeres en la Formación del Alma Americana.* Fundación Editorial El Perro y la Rana, 2016. https://albaciudad.org/wp-content/uploads/2021/05/influencia_de_las_mujeres_en_la_formacion_del_alma_americana.pdf.

De Zapata, Celia. "One Hundred Years of Women Writers in Latin America." *Latin American Literary Review* 3, no. 6 (1975): 7–16. JSTOR. http://www.jstor.org/stable/20118956.

Ibieta, Gabriella. "Teresa de la Parra." In *Spanish American Women Writers: A Bio-bibliographical Source Book*, edited by Doris E. Marting, 415–26. Greenwood Press, 1990.

Jehenson, Myriam Yvonne. "Teresa de la Parra." In *Latin-American Women Writers: Class, Race, and Gender*, 23–29. State University of New York Press, 1995.

Molloy, Sylvia. "Disappearing Acts: Reading Lesbian in Teresa de la Parra." In *¿Entiendes?: Queer Readings, Hispanic Writings*, edited by Emilie L. Bergmann and Paul Julian Smith, 230–56. Duke University Press, 1995.

Mueller, RoseAnna. *Teresa de la Parra: A Literary Life*. Cambridge Scholars, 2012.

Dorothy Shaver

"$110,000 Earned by Arkansas Girl: Dorothy Shaver, Who Climbed to Lord & Taylor Presidency, Received Sum in 1946." *New York Times*, June 24, 1947. ProQuest. https://search.proquest.com/docview/107897319.

Braun, Sandra Lee. *Forgotten First Lady: The Life, Rise, and Success of Dorothy Shaver, President of Lord & Taylor Department Store, and America's "First Lady of Retailing."* Doctoral dissertation, The University of Alabama, 2009. University of Alabama Repository. https://ir-api.ua.edu/api/core/bitstreams/2f45702c-2bd7-421d-9929-f346975a6a85/content.

Coogan, Hazel. "Dorothy Shaver (1893–1959)." *Encyclopedia of Arkansas*, January 18, 2017, https://encyclopediaofarkansas.net/entries/dorothy-shaver-1762/.

"Dorothy Shaver (1893–1959)." *Smithsonian Institution Archives*, 2002. http://amhistory.si.edu/archives/WIB-tour/dorothy_shaver.pdf.

"Miss Shaver Dead; Led Lord & Taylor." *New York Times*, June 29, 1959. ProQuest. https://search.proquest.com/docview/114774912.

Olsen, Kirstin. *Chronology of Women's History*, 261. Greenwood Press, 1994.

Perkins, Jeanne. "No. 1 Career Woman." *LIFE*, May 12, 1947: 117–28.

Dr. May Edward Chinn

Anderson, Gloria Long. "May Edward Chinn." In *Notable Black American Women*, edited by Jessie Carney Smith, 183–85. Gale Research, 1992.

Davis, George. "A Healing Hand in Harlem." *The New York Times*, April 22, 1979. ProQuest Historical Newspapers. https://search.proquest.com/historical-newspapers/healing-hand-harlem/docview/120893811/se-2.

Ennis, Thomas W. "Dr. May Edward Chinn, 84, Long a Harlem Physician." *The New York Times*, December 3, 1980. ProQuest Historical Newspapers. https://search.proquest.com/historical-newspapers/dr-may-edward-chinn-84-long-harlem-physician/docview/121366203/se-2.

Gamble, Vanessa N. "Chinn, May Edward." In *Notable American Women: A Biographical Dictionary, Completing the Twentieth Century*, edited by Susan Ware and Stacy Braukman, 118–19. Belknap Press, 2004.

Maurine Dallas Watkins

"Murder She Wrote." *Chicago Tribune*, July 16, 1997. https://www.chicagotribune.com/news/ct-xpm-1997-07-16-9707160264-story.html.

Perry, Douglas. *The Girls of Murder City: Fame, Lust, and the Beautiful Killers Who Inspired Chicago*. Penguin, 2011.

Poletika, Nicole. "Maurine Dallas Watkins: Sob Sisters, Pretty Demons, and All That Jazz." *Indiana Historical Bureau*, September 15, 2017. https://blog.history.in.gov/maurine-dallas-watkins-sob-sisters-pretty-demons-and-all-that-jazz/.

Rumore, Kori. "A Tribune Reporter Wrote the Hit Play 'Chicago' After Covering Cook County Murder Trials. Decades Later, We Owe Her an Obituary." *Chicago Tribune*, August 8, 2019. https://www.chicagotribune.com/entertainment/ct-ent-maurine-watkins-death-chicago-0811-20190808-brawaoyqvfgpfcllukd4z7riym-story.html.

Rumore, Kori, and Marianne Mather. *He Had It Coming: Four Murderous Women and the Reporter Who Immortalized Their Stories*. Agate Publishing, 2020.

Schiff, Judith Ann. "How Yale Begat Chicago." *Yale Alumni Magazine*, May/June 2012. https://yalealumnimagazine.com/articles/3439.

Chapter 3: Prioritizing Pursuits Other Than Marriage

Isotta Nogarola

Boršić, Luka, and Ivana Skuhala Karasman. "Isotta Nogarola—The Beginning of Gender Equality in Europe." *The Monist* 98, no. 1 (January 2015): 43–52. https://doi.org/10.1093/monist/onu006.

Brooklyn Museum. "Isotta Nogarola." www.brooklynmuseum.org/eascfa/dinner_party/heritage_floor/isotta_nogarola.

Jardine, Lisa. "Isotta Nogarola: Women Humanists—Education for What?" *History of Education* 12, no. 4 (1983): 231–44. doi:10.1080/0046760830120401.

Nogarola, Isotta, Margaret L. King, and Diana Robin. *Complete Writings: Letterbook, Dialogue on Adam and Eve, Orations*. University of Chicago Press, 2003.

Parker, Holt N. "Angela Nogarola (ca. 1400) and Isotta Nogarola (1418–1466): Thieves of Language." In *Women Writing Latin: From Roman Antiquity to Early Modern Europe*, edited by Laurie J. Churchill, Phyllis R. Brown, and Jane E. Jeffrey, 11–30. Routledge, 2002.

Mihrî Hatun

Andrews, Walter G., and Mehmet Kalpakli. "Ottoman Women Poets." In *The Age of Beloveds: Love and the Beloved in Early-Modern Ottoman and European Culture and Society*, 194–216. Duke University Press, 2005.

Gratien, Chris, host. Ottoman History Podcast. Episode, 357, "Love Poems of an Ottoman Woman: Mihrî Hatun with Didem Havlioğlu." April 12, 2018. http://www.ottomanhistorypodcast.com/2018/04/mihri-hatun.html.

Halman, Talat S., and Jayne L. Warner, eds. "At One Glance: Mihrî Hatun." In *Nightingales and Pleasure Gardens: Turkish Love Poems*, 35. Syracuse University Press, 2005.

Havlioğlu, Didem. "On the Margins and Between the Lines: Ottoman Women Poets from the Fifteenth to the Twentieth Centuries." *Turkish Historical Review* 1, no. 1 (2010): 25–54. doi:10.1163/187754610x494969.

———. *Mihrî Hatun: Performance, Gender-Bending, and Subversion in Ottoman Intellectual History*. Syracuse University Press, 2017.

Heath, Jennifer. "Mihrî Khatun." In *The Scimitar and the Veil: Extraordinary Women of Islam*, 420–21. HiddenSpring, 2004.

Reis, Huriye. "Medieval Women, Poetry, and Mihrî Hatun." *MANAS Journal of Social Studies* 10, no. 20, 147–57.

Silay, Kemal. "Singing His Words: Ottoman Women Poets and the Power of Patriarchy." In *Women in the Ottoman Empire: Middle Eastern Women in the Early Modern Era*, edited by Madeline Zilfi, 197–213. Brill, 1997.

Elena Lucrezia Cornaro Piscopia

Guernsey, Jane Howard. *The Lady Cornaro: Pride and Prodigy of Venice*. College Ave Press, 1999

Kessler, Ann. "Oblate and Heroine: Elena Lucrezia Scholastica Cornaro Piscopia (1646–1684)." In *Benedict in the World: Portraits of Monastic Oblates*, edited by Linda Kulzer and Roberta Bondi, 19–29. Liturgical Press, 2002.

Marie-Marguerite Biheron

Biheron, Marie Catherine. "To Benjamin Franklin from Marie Catherine Biheron, 10 September 1772." *Founders Online*. National Archives. https://founders.archives.gov/documents/Franklin/01-19-02-0199.

———. "To Benjamin Franklin from Marie Catherine Biheron, 10 October 1774." *Founders Online*. National Archives. https://founders.archives.gov/documents/Franklin/01-21-02-0174.

Boulinier, Georges. "Une Femme Anatomiste au Siècle des Lumières : Marie Marguerite Biheron (1719–1795)." *Histoire des Sciences Médicales* 35, no. 4 (2001): 411–23.

Burton, June K. *Napoleon and the Woman Question: Discourses of the Other Sex in French Education, Medicine, and Medical Law 1799–1815*, 81. Texas Tech University Press, 2007.

Gargam, Adeline. "Savoirs Mondains, Savoirs Savants: les Femmes et leurs Cabinets de Curiosités au Siècle des Lumières." *Genre & Histoire* 5 (2009).

Gelbart, Nina Rattner. "Adjusting the Lens: Locating Early Modern Women of Science." *Early Modern Women: An Interdisciplinary Journal* 11, no. 1 (2016): 116–27.

Jane Austen

"Jane Austen." *The British Library*, January 15, 2014. www.bl.uk/people/jane-austen.

Mullan, John. "Courtship, Love and Marriage in Jane Austen's Novels." *The British Library*, May 15, 2017. www.bl.uk/romantics-and-victorians/articles/courtship-love-and-marriage-in-jane-austens-novels.

O'Brien, Christopher. "Jane Austen's Early Death in the Context of Austen Family Mortality." *Persuasions: The Jane Austen Journal On-Line* 38, no. 1 (2017). JASNA. https://jasna.org/publications-2/persuasions-online/vol38no1/obrien.

Shields, Carol. *Jane Austen: A Life*. Penguin, 2005.

Florence Nightingale

Bostridge, Mark. *Florence Nightingale: The Making of an Icon*. Farrar, Straus and Giroux, 2008.

Cook, Edward Tyas. *The Life of Florence Nightingale*, vol. 2. Macmillan, 1914.

"Florence Nightingale Biography." *Florence Nightingale Museum*. https://www.florence-nightingale.co.uk/florence-nightingale-biography.

Karimi, Hosein, and Negin Masoudi Alavi. "Florence Nightingale: The Mother of Nursing." *Nursing and Midwifery Studies* 4, no. 2 (2015): e29475. doi:10.17795/nmsjournal29475.

Nightingale, Florence. *Ever yours, Florence Nightingale: Selected Letters*, edited by Martha Vicinus and Bea Nergaard. Harvard University Press, 1990.

Mary Cassatt

Chew, Elizabeth. "Mary Cassatt." *Smithsonian American Art Museum*. https://americanart.si.edu/artist/mary-cassatt-770.

Mathews, Nancy Mowll. *Mary Cassatt: A Life*. Yale University Press, 1998.

Edmonia Lewis

"Edmonia Lewis." *Smithsonian American Art Museum*. https://americanart.si.edu/artist/edmonia-lewis-2914.

Green, Penelope. "Overlooked No More: Edmonia Lewis, Sculptor of Worldwide Acclaim." *The New York Times*, July 25, 2018. https://www.nytimes.com/2018/07/25/obituaries/overlooked-edmonia-lewis-sculptor.html.

Henderson, Harry, and Albert Henderson. *The Indomitable Spirit of Edmonia Lewis*. Untreed Reads, 2012.

Tufts, Eleanor. "Edmonia Lewis." In *Our Hidden Heritage: Five Centuries of Women Artists*, 159–63. Paddington Press, 1974.

Tsuda Umeko

Furuki, Yoshiko. *The White Plum: A Biography of Ume Tsuda: Pioneer in the Higher Education of Japanese Women*. Weatherhill, 1991.

Iino, Masako. "From Japan to Bryn Mawr and Back." *Bryn Mawr College Bulletin*, 2019. https://www.brynmawr.edu/bulletin/japan-bryn-mawr-back.

Nimura, Janice P. *Daughters of the Samurai: A Journey from East to West and Back*. W. W. Norton & Company, 2016.

Tsuda, Umeko, and Yoshiko Furuki. *The Attic Letters: Ume Tsuda's Correspondence to Her American Mother*. Weatherhill, 1991.

Yamashiro, Amy D., and Ethel Ogane. "Tsuda Ume: Pioneering Education for Women and ELT." *The Language Teacher* 22, no. 5 (1998). JALT Publications. https://jalt-publications.org/old_tlt/files/98/may/yamashiro.html.

Marie Marvingt

Chahuneau, Louis. "Marie Marvingt, Pionnière de l'Aviation Tombée dans l'Oubli." *Le Point*, September 13, 2019. https://www.lepoint.fr/histoire/marie-marvingt-une-femme-d-exception-tombee-dans-l-oubli-13-09-2019-2335510_1615.php.

Lam, David. "Marie Marvingt 'la fiancée du danger' (1875–1963)." Monash University's CTIE, October 20, 2002. http://www.ctie.monash.edu.au/hargrave/marvingt.html.

Maggio, Rosalie. *Marie Marvingt, Fiancée of Danger: First Female Bomber Pilot, World-Class Athlete, and Inventor of the Air Ambulance*. McFarland, 2019.

Marvingt, Marie. "Leurs femmes." *La Vigie Marocaine*, October 22, 1934. Gallica. https://gallica.bnf.fr/ark:/12148/bpt6k2002342c/f2.item.zoom.

Anna May Wong

Chan, Anthony B. *Perpetually Cool: The Many Lives of Anna May Wong (1905–1961)*. Scarecrow Press, 2003.

Corliss, Richard. "Anna May Wong Did It Right." *Time*, January 29, 2005. http://content.time.com/time/arts/article/0,8599,1022536,00.html.

Gan, Geraldine. "Anna May Wong." In *Lives of Notable Asian Americans: Arts, Entertainment, Sports*, 83–91. Chelsea House Publishers, 1995.

Hodges, Graham Russell Gao. *Anna May Wong: From Laundryman's Daughter to Hollywood Legend*. Palgrave Macmillan, 2004.

Liu, Cynthia W. "When Dragon Ladies Die, Do They Come Back as Butterflies? Re-Imagining Anna May Wong." In *Countervisions: Asian American Film Criticism*, edited by Darrell Y. Hamamoto and Sandra Liu, 23–38. Temple University Press, 2000.

Zia, Helen, and Susan B. Gall, eds. "Anna May Wong." In *Notable Asian Americans*, 414–16. Gale Research, 1995.

Keiko Fukuda

Keiko Fukada Judo Foundation. "Shihan Keiko Fukuda." http://www.keikofukudajudofoundation.org/?page_id=5.

"Mrs. Judo Movie." *Mrs. Judo: Be Strong, Be Gentle, Be Beautiful*. www.mrsjudomovie.com.

Romer, Yuriko G., dir. *Mrs. Judo: Be Strong, Be Gentle, Be Beautiful*. United States/Japan: Zoetrope Aubry Productions, 2012.

Yardley, William. "Keiko Fukuda, a Trailblazer in Judo, Dies at 99." *The New York Times*, February 16, 2013. https://www.nytimes.com/2013/02/17/sports/keiko-fukuda-99-a-trailblazer-in-judo-is-dead.html.

Dr. Sivaramakrishna Iyer Padmavati

Dutt, Anonna. "Legendary Cardio Specialist Dr Sivaramakrishna Iyer Padmavati Dies of Covid-19 at 103." *Hindustan Times*, August 31, 2020. https://www.hindustantimes.com/cities/legendary-cardio-specialist-dr-sivaramakrishna-iyer-padmavati-dies-of-covid-at-103/story-XYGFBcz9oGq8Qj9j0o0xzL.html.

N. P., Ullekh. "Dr. S Padmavati: India's First & Oldest Woman Heart Specialist." *The Economic Times*, July 1, 2013. https://economictimes.indiatimes.com/dr-s-padmavati-indias-first-oldest-woman-heart-specialist/articleshow/20855888.cms.

Padmavati, Sivaramakrishna. "Eminent Indians in Medicine." *National Medical Journal of India* 1, no. 3 (1988): 157–60. NMJI Archive. https://nmji.in/nmji/approval/archive/Volume-1/Volume-1-Issue-3.html.

———. *My Life and Medicine*. Notion Press, 2018.

Yadava, O. P. "The Heart Doctor with a Big Heart Passes Away." *The Times of India*, August 31, 2020. https://timesofindia.indiatimes.com/india/the-heart-doctor-with-a-big-heart-passes-away/articleshow/77841582.cms.

Chapter 4: The Freedom of Single Life

Anna Bijns

Aercke, Kristiaan. "Anna Bijns: Germanic Sappho." In *Women Writers of the Renaissance and Reformation*, edited by Katharina M. Wilson, 365–97. University of Georgia Press, 1987.

———. "Word as Weapon in a Holy Mission: Anna Bijns." In *Women's Writing from the Low Countries 1200–1875: A Bilingual Anthology*, edited by Lia van Gemert et al., 160–75. Amsterdam University Press, 2010.

Keßler, Judith. "'Please Do Not Mind the Crudeness of Its Weave': Literature, Gender and the Polemic Authority of Anna Bijns." In *Literary Cultures and Public Opinion in the Low Countries, 1450–1650*, edited by Jan Bloemendal, Arjan van Dixhoorn, and Elsa Strietman, 55–89. Brill, 2011.

Welsh, Jennifer L. "Bijns, Anna." In *Encyclopedia of Martin Luther and the Reformation*, edited by Mark A. Lamport, 73–75. Rowman & Littlefield, 2017.

Gabrielle Suchon

Broad, Jacqueline and Karen Green, eds. "Women of Late Seventeenth-Century France." In *A History of Women's Political Thought in Europe, 1400–1700*, 255–64. Cambridge University Press, 2009.

Desnain, Véronique. "Gabrielle Suchon: Militant Philosophy in Seventeenth-Century France." *Forum for Modern Language Studies* 49, no. 3 (July 2013): 257–71. https://doi.org/10.1093/fmls/cqs030.

Le Dœuff, Michèle, and Penelope Deutscher. "Feminism Is Back in France: Or Is It?" *Hypatia* 15, no. 4 (2000): 243–55. JSTOR. http://www.jstor.org/stable/3810690.

Papillon, Philibert. "Gabrielle Suchon." In *Bibliothèque des Auteurs de Bourgogne*, 298–99. François Desventes, 1745. Gallica. https://gallica.bnf.fr/ark:/12148/bpt6k10434099/f308.image.

Stanton, Domna C. "The Female Mind Reformed: Pedagogical Counter-Discourses, Radical and Regressive, under Louis XIV." In *The Dynamics of Gender in Early Modern France: Women Writ, Women Writing*, 89–119. Ashgate Publishing, 2014.

Suchon, Gabrielle. *A Woman Who Defends All the Persons of Her Sex: Selected Philosophical and Moral Writings*. Edited and translated by Domna C. Stanton and Rebecca M. Wilkin. University of Chicago Press, 2010.

Susan B. Anthony

Barry, Kathleen. *Susan B. Anthony: A Biography of a Singular Feminist*. New York University Press, 1988.

Bly, Nellie. "Champion of Her Sex: Miss Susan B. Anthony Tells the Story of Her Remarkable Life to 'Nellie Bly.'" *The World*, February 2, 1896. http://suffrageandthemedia.org/wp-content/uploads/2017/05/BLY-NYWorld2Feb1896p10.jpg.

Faderman, Lillian. "The Loves and Living Arrangements of Nineteenth-Century Suffrage Leaders." In *To Believe in Women: What Lesbians Have Done for America—A History*, 15–39. Houghton Mifflin Harcourt, 2000.

Harper, Judith E. "Biography." *PBS*. https://www.pbs.org/kenburns/not-for-ourselves-alone/biography.

National Park Service. "Susan B. Anthony." https://www.nps.gov/people/susan-b-anthony.htm.

National Women's Hall of Fame. "Susan B. Anthony." https://www.womenofthehall.org/inductee/susan-b-anthony/.

Louisa May Alcott

Alcott, Louisa May. *Louisa May Alcott: Her Life, Letters, and Journals*, edited by Ednah D. Cheney. Little, Brown, and Company, 1898. Project Gutenberg. https://www.gutenberg.org/files/38049/38049-h/38049-h.htm.

———. "Happy Women." In *Short Stories*, edited by Candace Ward. Dover Publications, 1996.

———. *Alternative Alcott*. Edited by Elaine Showalter. Rutgers University Press, 1997.

"Alcott: 'Not the Little Woman You Thought She Was.'" *NPR*, December 28, 2009. https://www.npr.org/templates/story/story.php?storyId=121831612.

Graham, Beckett, and Susan Vollenweider, hosts. The History Chicks. "Episode 104: Louisa May Alcott." April 8, 2018. Podcast. https://thehistorychicks.com/episode-104-louisa-may-alcott/.

Hirschhorn, Norbert, and Ian Greaves. "Louisa May Alcott: Her Mysterious Illness." *Perspectives in Biology and Medicine* 50, no. 2 (2007): 243–59. Project MUSE. https://dx.doi.org/10.1353/pbm.2007.0019.

Norwood, Arlisha R. "Louisa May Alcott." National Women's History Museum. https://www.womenshistory.org/education-resources/biographies/louisa-may-alcott.

"The Two Loves of Louisa May Alcott." New England Historical Society, 2019. https://www.newenglandhistoricalsociety.com/two-loves-louisa-may-alcott/.

Ida M. Tarbell

King, Gilbert. "The Woman Who Took on the Tycoon." *Smithsonian Magazine*, July 5, 2012. https://www.smithsonianmag.com/history/the-woman-who-took-on-the-tycoon-651396/.

Kochersberger, Robert C., ed. *More Than a Muckraker: Ida Tarbell's Lifetime in Journalism.* University of Tennessee Press, 1994.

Lowrie, Arthur L. "Brief Biography and Bibliography, Ida M. Tarbell: Investigative Journalist Par Excellence." Allegheny College. https://sites.allegheny.edu/tarbell/briefbio/.

Piascik, Andy. "Ida Tarbell: The Woman Who Took on Standard Oil." *Connecticut History*, January 6, 2022. https://connecticuthistory.org/ida-tarbell-the-woman-who-took-on-standard-oil/.

Schlipp, Madelon G., and Sharon Murphy, eds. "Ida Minerva Tarbell." In *Great Women of the Press*, 103–11. Southern Illinois University Press, 1983.

Tarbell, Ida. *All in the Day's Work: An Autobiography.* Macmillan, 1939.

Edith Maude Eaton a.k.a. Sui Sin Far

Far, Sui Sin. "Leaves from the Mental Portfolio of an Eurasian." *Quotidiana*, June 1, 2008. https://essays.quotidiana.org/far/leaves_mental_portfolio/.

Ling, Amy. "Edith Eaton: Pioneer Chinamerican Writer and Feminist." *American Literary Realism, 1870–1910* 16, no. 2 (1983): 287–98. JSTOR. http://www.jstor.org/stable/27746105.

———. "Edith Maud Eaton (Sui Sin Far) (1865–1914)." Georgetown University. https://faculty.georgetown.edu/bassr/heath/syllabuild/iguide/eaton.html.

McMullen, Lorraine. "Eaton, Edith Maud." *The Dictionary of Canadian Biography*, 14. University of Toronto/Université Laval, 1998. https://www.biographi.ca/en/bio/eaton_edith_maud_14E.html.

Ng, Franklin. "Edith Maud Eaton." In *Distinguished Asian Americans: A Biographical Dictionary*, edited by Hyung-chan Kim, 91–93. Greenwood Press, 1999.

White-Parks, Annette. *Sui Sin Far / Edith Maude Eaton: A Literary Biography.* University of Illinois Press, 1995.

Alma W. Thomas

Fine, Elsa Honig. "Alma Thomas." In *The Afro-American Artist: A Search for Identity*, 151–53. Hacker Art Books, 1982.

Munro, Eleanor. "Alma W. Thomas." In *Originals: American Women Artists*, 189–97. Simon & Schuster, 1979.

National Museum of Women in the Arts. "Alma Woodsey Thomas." https://nmwa.org/art/artists/alma-woodsey-thomas/.

Smithsonian American Art Museum. Markoski, Katherine. "Alma Thomas." https://americanart.si.edu/artist/alma-thomas-4778.

Chapter 5: Criticisms of Marriage as an Institution

Madeleine de Scudéry

Aronson, Nicole. *Mademoiselle de Scudéry.* Translated by Stuart R. Aronson. Twayne Publishers, 1978.

Conley, John. "Madeleine de Scudéry." *The Stanford Encyclopedia of Philosophy* (Fall 2019 Edition). https://plato.stanford.edu/entries/madeleine-scudery/#Biog.

Garnett, Mary Anne. "Madeleine de Scudéry: Les Femmes Illustres ou les Harangues Héroïques (1642)." In *Writings by Pre-Revolutionary French Women*, edited by Colette H. Winn and Anne R. Larsen, 243–56. Routledge, 2017.

Harth, Erica. "Cartesian Women." *Yale French Studies*, no. 80 (1991): 146–64. JSTOR. https://doi.org/10.2307/2930265.

Scudéry, Madeleine de. *Mademoiselle de Scudéry: sa vie et sa correspondance.* Edited by Edmé-Jacques-Benoît Rathery and Boutron. Léon Techener, 1873.

———. *The Story of Sapho.* Edited and translated by Karen Newman. University of Chicago Press, 2003.

Tebben, Maryann. "Speaking of Women: Molière and Conversation at the Court of Louis XIV." *Modern Language Studies* 29, no. 2 (1999): 189–207. JSTOR. https://doi.org/10.2307/3195414.

Hannah Griffitts

Blecki, Catherine La Courreye, and Karin A. Wulf, eds. "Hannah Griffitts." In *Milcah Martha Moore's Book: A Commonplace Book from Revolutionary America*, xvii. Pennsylvania State University Press, 2007.

Stabile, Susan M. "Introduction." In *Memory's Daughters: The Material Culture of Remembrance in Eighteenth-Century America*, 10. Cornell University Press, 2004.

Wulf, Karin A. "Despise the Mean Distinctions [These] Times Have Made: The Complexity of Patriotism and Quaker Loyalism in One Pennsylvania Family." *H-Net: Humanities & Social Sciences Online.* https://revolution.h-net.msu.edu/essays/wulf.html.

———. *Not All Wives: Women of Colonial Philadelphia*, 16, 41, 45–48, 54, 65–67, 108, 138, 182–86. Cornell University Press, 2000.

Maria Edgeworth

Botkin, Frances R. "Finding Her Own Voice or 'Being on Her Own Bottom': A Community of Women in Maria Edgeworth's *Helen*." In *New Essays on Maria Edgeworth*, edited by Julie Nash, 93–108. Routledge, 2018.

Butler, Marilyn. *Maria Edgeworth: A Literary Biography.* Oxford University Press, 1972.

Barbara Hillary

"Barbara Hillary." https://barbarahillary.com/about/.

Collins, Lauren. "The Latest Dreams of Barbara Hillary, the First African American Woman to Travel to the North Pole." *The New Yorker*, July 26, 2019. https://www.newyorker.com/culture/culture-desk/the-latest-dreams-of-barbara-hillary-the-first-african-american-woman-to-travel-to-the-north-pole.

Katz, Brigit. "Barbara Hillary, a Pioneering African American Adventurer, Dies at 88." *Smithsonian Magazine*, November 27, 2019. https://www.smithsonianmag.com/smart-news/barbara-hillary-pioneering-african-american-adventurer-has-died-180973663/.

Kay, Laura. "What It Takes to Get There: An Interview with Barbara Hillary." *The Scholar & Feminist Online*, June 17, 2008. Barnard Center for Research on Women. https://sfonline.barnard.edu/ice/hillary_01.htm.

Knapp, Shelby. "Barbara Hillary: Our Favorite Boundary Breaker." *REI Blog*, March 3, 2017. Internet Archive. https://web.archive.org/web/20230610111830/https://www.rei.com/blog/snowsports/barbara-hillary-favorite-boundary-breaker.

"New School Alumna Barbara Hillary, the First African American Woman to Reach the North Pole, Dies at 88." *New School News*, November 27, 2019. https://blogs.newschool.edu/news/2019/11/new-school-alumna-barbara-hillary-the-first-african-american-woman-to-reach-the-north-pole-dies-at-88/.

Nabawiyya Musa

Badran, Margot. "Expressing Feminism and Nationalism in Autobiography: The Memoirs of an Egyptian Educator." In *De/colonizing the Subject: The Politics of Gender in Women's Autobiography*, edited by Sidonie Smith and Julia Watson, 270–96. University of Minnesota Press, 1992.

———. *Feminists, Islam, and Nation: Gender and the Making of Modern Egypt.* Princeton University Press, 1995.

Civantos, Christina. "Reading and Writing the Turn-of-the-Century Egyptian Woman Intellectual: Nabawiyya Musa's *Ta'rikhi Bi-Qalami.*" *Journal of Middle East Women's Studies* 9, no. 2 (2013): 4–31. https://doi.org/10.2979/jmiddeastwomstud.9.2.4.

Elsadda, Hoda. "Nabawiya Musa." In *Arab Women Writers: A Critical Reference Guide, 1873–1999*, edited by Radwa Ashour, Ferial J. Ghazoul, Hasna Reda-Mekdashi, and translated by Mandy McClure, 112–14. The American University in Cairo Press, 2008.

Photograph of the Egyptian Delegates [Nabawiyya Musa, Huda Sha'arawi, and Saiza Nabarawi], 1920, C. C. Catt Collection, Bryn Mawr College Library. http://triptych.brynmawr.edu/cdm/singleitem/collection/suffragists/id/530.

Vezzadini, Elena. "Musa, Nabawiyya." In *Dictionary of African Biography*, edited by Emmanuel Akyeampong and Henry Louis Gates, 342–44. Oxford University Press, 2012.

Nadia Boulanger

Brooks, Jeanice. "Noble et Grande Servante de La Musique: Telling the Story of Nadia Boulanger's Conducting Career." *The Journal of Musicology* 14, no. 1 (1996): 92–116. https://doi.org/10.2307/763959.

Burton-Hill, Clemency. "The Greatest Music Teacher Who Ever Lived." *BBC Culture*, April 19, 2017. https://www.bbc.com/culture/article/20170308-the-greatest-music-teacher-who-ever-lived.

Hughes, Allen. "Nadia Boulanger, Teacher of Top Composers, Dies." *The New York Times*, October 23, 1979. https://www.nytimes.com/1979/10/23/archives/nadia-boulanger-teacher-of-top-composers-dies-onewoman-graduate.html.

Rorem, Ned. "The Composer and the Music Teacher." *The New York Times*, May 23, 1982. https://www.nytimes.com/1982/05/23/books/the-composer-and-the-music-teacher.html.

Rosenstiel, Léonie. *Nadia Boulanger: A Life in Music.* W. W. Norton, 1982.

Sadie Delany and Bessie Delany

Delany, Sarah L., A. Elizabeth Delany, and Amy Hill Hearth. *Having Our Say: The Delany Sisters' First 100 Years.* Dell, 1994.

Yoshiya Nobuko

Hanawa, Yukiko. "The Story of Yoshiya Nobuko." In *A Queer World: The Center for Lesbian and Gay Studies Reader*, edited by Martin Duberman, 51–52. New York University Press, 1997.

Robertson, Jennifer. "Yoshiya Nobuko: Out and Outspoken in Practice and Prose." In *Same-Sex Cultures and Sexualities: An Anthropological Reader*, 196–211. Blackwell Publishing, 2005.

Suzuki, Michiko. "Yoshiya Nobuko and the Romance of Sisterhood." In *Becoming Modern Women: Love and Female Identity in Prewar Japanese Literature and Culture*, 34–62. Stanford University Press, 2009.

"Yoshiya Nobuko." In *Japanese Women Novelists in the 20th Century: 104 Biographies, 1900–1993*, edited by Sachiko Shibata Schierbeck and Marlene R. Edelstein, 88–92. Museum Tusculanum Press, 1994.

Yoshiya, Nobuko. *Yellow Rose.* Translated by Sarah Frederick. 2nd ed. Expanded Editions Press, 2016.

Chapter 6: Advocating for Oneself

Margaret Brent

Carr, Lois G. "Margaret Brent—A Brief History." Maryland State Archives, February 7, 2002. https://msa.maryland.gov/msa/speccol/sc3500/sc3520/002100/002177/html/mbrent2.html.

Davis, Jennifer. "Margaret Brent, Lord Baltimore's Legal Representative." *Library of Congress Blog*, January 23, 2017. https://blogs.loc.gov/law/2017/01/margaret-brent-lord-baltimores-legal-representative/.

Krismann, Carol. "Brent, Margaret (1601–1671), Land Proprietor, Lawyer." In *Encyclopedia of American Women in Business*, vol. 1, 91–93. Greenwood Press, 2005.

Masson, Margaret W. "Margaret Brent, c. 1601–c. 1671, Lawyer, Landholder-Entrepreneur." In *Notable Maryland Women*, edited by Winifred G. Helmes, 43–46. Tidewater Publishers, 1977.

Sor Juana Inés de la Cruz

De la Cruz, Juana Inés. "You Foolish Men." *Poets.org*. Academy of American Poets. https://poets.org/poem/you-foolish-men.

Kantaris, Geoffrey. "Sor Juana Inés de la Cruz (Juana Ramírez de Asbaje)." *Latin American Studies at Cambridge*. https://web.archive.org/web/20190430044434/http://www.latin-american.cam.ac.uk/culture/SorJuana/.

Morkovsky, Mary Christine. "Sor Juana Inés de la Cruz." In *A History of Women Philosophers: Modern Women Philosophers, 1600–1900,* edited by Mary Ellen Waithe, vol. 3, 59–72. Springer Science + Business Media, 1991.

Paz, Octavio. *Sor Juana, or, The Traps of Faith.* Belknap Press, 1990.

"Sor Juana Inés de la Cruz's Letter to Sor Filotea (1691)." In *Colonial Spanish America: A Documentary History,* edited by Kenneth Mills, William B. Taylor, and Sandra Lauderdale Graham, 207–14. Rowman & Littlefield, 2002.

Sarah Moore Grimké

Bartlett, Elizabeth Ann. "Sarah Grimké." In *Liberty, Equality, Sorority: The Origins and Interpretation of American Feminist Thought: Frances Wright, Sarah Grimké, and Margaret Fuller,* 57–87. Carlson Publishing, 1994.

Gattozzi, Patrice, and Peter Brown. "1870 Women's March and Vote." Hyde Park Historical Society. https://www.hydeparkhistoricalsociety.org/1870-womens-march-and-vote/.

Grimké, Sarah. *Letters on the Equality of the Sexes and the Condition of Women.* Isaac Knapp, 1838. Project Gutenberg. https://www.gutenberg.org/cache/epub/69485/pg69485-images.html.

Lerner, Gerda. *The Grimké Sisters from South Carolina: Pioneers for Women's Rights and Abolition.* Schocken Books, 1971.

National Women's Hall of Fame. "Sarah Grimké." https://www.womenofthehall.org/inductee/sarah-grimk/.

Henriette DeLille

Clark, Emily, and Virginia M. Gould. "The Feminine Face of Afro-Catholicism in New Orleans, 1727–1852." *The William and Mary Quarterly* 59, no. 2 (2002): 409–48. JSTOR. https://doi.org/10.2307/3491743.

Gould, Virginia M. "Henriette Delille, Free Women of Color, and Catholicism in Antebellum New Orleans, 1727–1852." In *Beyond Bondage: Free Women of Color in the Americas*, edited by David Barry Gaspar and Darlene Clark Hine, 271–85. University of Illinois Press, 2004.

Porche-Frilot, Donna Marie. "Propelled by Faith: Henriette Delille and the Literacy Practices of Black Women Religious in Antebellum New Orleans." PhD diss., Louisiana State University Graduate School, 2005. https://digitalcommons.lsu.edu/gradschool_dissertations/2418.

Sisters of the Holy Family. "Venerable Henriette Delille, 1812–1862: 'Servant of Slaves.'" https://www.sistersoftheholyfamily.com/henriette-delille/.

Cornelia Sorabji

"Alumna: Cornelia Sorabji." *University of Oxford Faculty of Law*, November 20, 2018. https://www.law.ox.ac.uk/content/alumna-cornelia-sorabji-1866-1954.

Basu, Aparna. "Cornelia Sorabji: India's Pioneer Woman Lawyer, A Biography." *Indian Historical Review* 34, no. 2 (2007): 248–51. https://doi.org/10.1177/037698360703400227.

Sommerlad, Joe. "Cornelia Sorabji: Who Was India's First Female Lawyer?" *The Independent*, November 15, 2017. https://www.independent.co.uk/news/world/asia/cornelia-sorabji-india-female-lawyer-first-woman-google-doodle-feminism-oxford-university-a8055916.html.

Sorabji, Richard. *Opening Doors: The Untold Story of Cornelia Sorabji, Reformer, Lawyer, and Champion of Women's Rights in India.* I. B. Tauris, 2010.

———. "Opening Doors: The Untold Story of Cornelia Sorabji, Reformer, Lawyer and Champion of Women's Rights in India." Gresham College, June 17, 2010. https://www.gresham.ac.uk/lecture/transcript/print/opening-doors-the-untold-story-of-cornelia-sorabji-reformer-lawyer-and-champion/.

Lyda B. Conley

Berry, Dawn Bradley. "Lyda Burton Conley." In *50 Most Influential Women in American Law*, 43–45. Lowell House, 1996.

Dayton, Kim. "'Trespassers, Beware!': Lyda Burton Conley and the Battle for Huron Place Cemetery." *Yale Journal of Law and Feminism* 8, no. 1 (1995):

1–30. Yale Law School Journals. https://openyls.law.yale.edu/bitstream/handle/20.500.13051/7208/05_8YaleJL_Feminism1_1996_.pdf.

Flinn, Kara Evans. "Lyda Conley: Wyandot Guardian and Lawyer." *Kansas City Public Library Local History Blog*, April 5, 2018. https://kchistory.org/blog/lyda-conley-wyandot-guardian-and-lawyer.

Sophia Duleep Singh

Anand, Anita. *Sophia: Princess, Suffragette, Revolutionary*. Bloomsbury, 2015.

———, host. *Sophia: Suffragette Princess*. Produced by Anna Cox and Aaqil Ahmed. 2015. *BBC*. https://www.bbc.co.uk/programmes/b06qnnyp.

Hampton Court Palace. "Sophia Duleep Singh." https://www.hrp.org.uk/hampton-court-palace/history-and-stories/sophia-duleep-singh/.

Mukherjee, Sumita. "Herabai Tata and Sophia Duleep Singh: Suffragette Resistances for India and Britain, 1910–1920." In *South Asian Resistances in Britain 1858–1947*, edited by Mukherjee and Rehana Ahmed, 106–21. Bloomsbury Publishing, 2011.

Visram, Rozina. "Sophia Duleep Singh." In *Asians in Britain: 400 Years of History*, 164–68. Pluto Press, 2002.

Maggie Kuhn

Kuhn, Maggie, Christina Long, and Laura Quinn. *No Stone Unturned: The Life and Times of Maggie Kuhn*. Ballantine Books, 1991.

Gerty Archimède

Davis, Angela Y. *Angela Davis: An Autobiography*, 215–16. International, 1988.

Franceinfo. "La Députée Guadeloupéenne Gerty Archimède Était l'Amour Caché du Président Ivoirien Félix Houphouët-Boigny." June 2, 2019. https://la1ere.francetvinfo.fr/martinique/deputee-guadeloupeenne-gerty-archimede-etait-amour-cache-du-president-ivoirien-felix-houphouet-boigny-716831.html.

Joseph-Gabriel, Annette K. "Gerty Archimède and the Struggle for Decolonial Citizenship in the French Antilles, 1946–51." In *Black French Women and the Struggle for Equality, 1848–2016*, edited by Félix Germain and Silyane Larcher, 89–106. University of Nebraska Press, 2018.

———. *Reimagining Liberation: How Black Women Transformed Citizenship in the French Empire*, 14, 73–74, 78–79, 194. University of Illinois Press, 2019.

Région Guadeloupe. "2019 Année Gerty Archimède." https://www.regionguadeloupe.fr/fileadmin/Site_Region_Guadeloupe/Mediatheque/Brochures_et_publications/2019_Brochure_Gerty_Archimeede_21012020_web.pdf.

Dulcie September

Albin, Claire. "Biography of Dulcie September." *South African History Online*, February 8, 2021. https://www.sahistory.org.za/archive/biography-dulcie-september-claire-albin.

Bundy, Colin. "South Africa's African National Congress in Exile." *Oxford Research Encyclopedia of African History*, April 26, 2018. https://oxfordre.com/africanhistory/view/10.1093/acrefore/9780190277734.001.0001/acrefore-9780190277734-e-81.

Dérens, Jacqueline. "La Vie de Dulcie September | Jacqueline Dérens | UPA." Virtual lecture. Posted March 20, 2018, by Université Populaire d'Arcueil. YouTube, 1:59:11. https://www.youtube.com/watch?v=BrX82EkkpC4.

Navarre, Jean-Philippe, director. *Dulcie September, Affaire Non Classée*. Produced by Michel Pomarède. *France Culture*, October 2017. https://www.radiofrance.fr/franceculture/podcasts/une-histoire-particuliere-un-recit-documentaire-en-deux-parties/une-militante-qui-en-savait-trop-5611696.

Nelson Mandela Foundation. "The First Dulcie September Annual Lecture." March 2, 2021, https://www.nelsonmandela.org/news/entry/the-first-dulcie-september-annual-lecture.

Newton, Michael. "Dulcie September." In *Famous Assassinations in World History: An Encyclopedia*, vol. 1, 520–22. ABC-CLIO, 2014.

Chapter 7: Creating a Sense of Community Outside the Nuclear Family

The Beguines

Bennett, Judith M., and Amy M. Froide, eds. *Singlewomen in the European Past, 1250–1800*, 11–12, 86–87, 93, 193. University of Pennsylvania Press, 2013.

De Moor, Tine. "Single, Safe, and Sorry? Explaining the Early Modern Beguine Movement in the Low Countries." *Journal of Family History* 39, no. 1 (2014): 3–21.

Hirbodian, Sigrid. "Religious Women: Secular Canonesses and Beguines." In *The Oxford Handbook of Christian Monasticism*, edited by Bernice M. Kaczynski and Thomas Sullivan, 285–99. Oxford University Press, 2020.

Lehmijoki-Gardner, Maiju. "Laywomen, Religious." In *Women and Gender in Medieval Europe: An Encyclopedia*, vol. 14, edited by Margaret Schaus, 462–63. Taylor & Francis, 2006.

Miller, Tanya Stabler. *The Beguines of Medieval Paris: Gender, Patronage, and Spiritual Authority*. University of Pennsylvania Press, 2014.

Simons, Walter. *Cities of Ladies: Beguine Communities in the Medieval Low Countries, 1200–1565*. University of Pennsylvania Press, 2001.

Anna Maria van Schurman

Irwin, Joyce L. "Learned Woman of Utrecht, Anna Maria van Schurman." In *Women Writers of the 17th Century,* edited by Katharina M. Wilson and Frank J. Warnke, 164–85. University of Georgia Press, 1989.

Larsen, Anne R. "A Women's Republic of Letters: Anna Maria van Schurman, Marie de Gournay, and Female Self-Representation in Relation to the Public Sphere." *Early Modern Women* 3 (2008): 105–26. JSTOR. https://www.jstor.org/stable/23541520.

Pal, Carol. "Marie de Gournay, Marie du Moulin, and Anna Maria van Schurman: Constructing Intellectual Kinship." In *Republic of Women: Rethinking the Republic of Letters in the Seventeenth Century,* 78–109. Cambridge University Press, 2012.

Van Beek, Pieta. *The First Female University Student: Anna Maria van Schurman (1636).* Igitur, 2010.

The Ladies of *Millenium Hall*

Elliott, Dorice Williams. "Sarah Scott's *Millenium Hall* and Female Philanthropy." *Studies in English Literature, 1500–1900* 35, no. 3 (1995): 535–53. JSTOR. https://doi.org/10.2307/450896.

Rizzo, Betty. "Reformers: Sarah Scott and Barbara Montagu." In *Companions Without Vows: Relationships Among Eighteenth-Century British Women,* 295–319. University of Georgia Press, 2008.

Scott, Sarah. *A Description of Millenium Hall and the Country Adjacent.* J. Newbury, 1762. Project Gutenberg. https://www.gutenberg.org/files/26050/26050-h/26050-h.htm.

Smith, Johanna M. "Philanthropic Community in *Millenium Hall* and the York Ladies Committee." *The Eighteenth Century* 36, no. 3 (1995): 266–82. JSTOR. http://www.jstor.org/stable/41467794.

Margaretta Forten

Brown, Ira. "Cradle of Feminism: The Philadelphia Female Anti-Slavery Society, 1833–1840." *The Pennsylvania Magazine of History and Biography* 102, no. 2 (1978): 143–66. JSTOR. https://www.jstor.org/stable/20091253.

Maillard, Mary. *Whispers of Cruel Wrongs: The Correspondence of Louisa Jacobs and Her Circle, 1879–1911.* University of Wisconsin Press, 2017.

Rachlin, Morgan. "Biographical Sketch of Margaretta Forten, 1806–1875." In *Online Biographical Dictionary of the Woman Suffrage Movement in the United States,* edited by Kathryn Kish Sklar and Thomas Dublin. Alexander Street, 2018. https://documents.alexanderstreet.com/d/1007600738.

Sumler-Lewis, Janice. "The Forten-Purvis Women of Philadelphia and the American Anti-Slavery Crusade." *The Journal of Negro History* 66, no. 4 (1981): 281–88. JSTOR. https://www.jstor.org/stable/2717236.

Winch, Julie. "Margaretta Forten (1808–1875)." *In Notable Black American Women*, edited by Jessie Carney Smith, 354–58. Gale Research, 1992.

———. "'You Have Talents—Only Cultivate Them': Philadelphia's Black Female Literacy Societies and the Abolitionist Crusade." In *The Abolitionist Sisterhood*, edited by Jean Fagan Yellin and John C. Van Horne, 105–17. Cornell University Press, 1994.

Dorothy Irene Height

Crewe, Sandra Edmonds. "Dorothy Irene Height: Profile of a Giant in Pursuit of Equal Justice for Black Women." *Affilia* 24, no. 2 (2009): 199–205. SAGE Journals. https://doi.org/10.1177/0886109909331753.

Fox, Margalit. "Dorothy Height, Largely Unsung Giant of the Civil Rights Era, Dies at 98." *The New York Times,* April 20, 2010. https://www.nytimes.com/2010/04/21/us/21height.html.

Height, Dorothy I. *Open Wide the Freedom Gates: A Memoir*. Public Affairs, 2003.

National Park Service. "Dorothy I. Height." www.nps.gov/people/dorothy-i-height.htm.

Norwood, Arlisha. "Dorothy Height." National Women's History Museum. www.womenshistory.org/education-resources/biographies/dorothy-height.

Chapter 8: Single Women in Positions of Power as Heads of State

Seondeok

Bae-yong, Lee. "Queen Seondeok Paves the Road to Unification." In *Women in Korean History*, translated by Lee Kyong-hee, 137–40. Ewha Womans University Press, 2008.

Hwang, Kyung Moon. "Queen Seondeok and Silla's Unification of Korea." In *A History of Korea,* 2nd ed., 12–21. Palgrave Macmillan, 2017.

Jung, Hyang-jin, et al., editors. "Queen Seondeok: Korea's First Female Leader." In *The Practice of Hongik Ingan: Lives of Queen Seondeok, Shin Saimdang and Yi Yulgok*, 9–31. Diamond Sutra Recitation Group, 2011.

Lee, Soyoung, and Denise Patry Leidy. *Silla: Korea's Golden Kingdom*, 22. Metropolitan Museum of Art, 2013.

"Queen Seondeok." In *Encyclopedia of Korean Folk Literature,* vol. 3, edited by Chung Myung-sub, translated by Jung Ha-yun, 193. National Folk Museum of Korea, 2014.

Kōken

Aoki, Michiko Y. "Kōken-Shōtoku Tennō (718–70; 46th; r. 749–58; and 48th; r. 764–70)." In *Heroic with Grace: Legendary Women of Japan,* edited by Chieko Irie Mulhern, 70–74. M. E. Sharpe, 1991.

Deal, William E., and Brian Ruppert. *A Cultural History of Japanese Buddhism.* John Wiley & Sons, 2015.

Friday, Karl F., editor. *Japan Emerging: Premodern History to 1850*. Routledge, 2012.

Johnson, L. L. "Kōken-Shōtoku." In *Women in World History: A Biographical Encyclopedia*, vol. 8, edited by Anne Commire and Deborah Klezmer, 753–54. Yorkin Publications, 2000.

Kōjirō, Naoki. "The Nara State: Authority Crisis." In *The Cambridge History of Japan*, vol. 1, edited by Delmer Brown, translated by Felicia G. Bock, 257–65. Cambridge University Press, 1993.

Little, Lester K. "Cypress Beams, Kufic Script, and Cut Stone: Rebuilding the Master Narrative of European History." *Speculum* 79, no. 4 (2004): 909–10. JSTOR. http://www.jstor.org/stable/20463062.

The British Library. "The Million Pagoda Charms." www.bl.uk/collection-items/one-million-pagoda-charm.

"Window to a Rising Sun." *Chicago Tribune*, June 22, 1986. https://www.chicagotribune.com/news/ct-xpm-1986-06-22-8602140619-story.html.

Sitt al-Mulk

Baker, Christine D. "Sitt al-Mulk." In *The Dictionary of African Biography*, edited by Emmanuel Kwaku Akyeampong and Henry Louis Gates Jr., 404–5. Oxford University Press, 2011.

Brett, Michael. *The Fatimid Empire*, 97. Edinburgh University Press, 2017.

Cortese, Delia. "Sitt al-Mulk." In *The Oxford Encyclopedia of Women in World History*, vol. 1, edited by Bonnie G. Smith, 53–54. Oxford University Press, 2008.

Cortese, Delia, and Simonetta Calderini. "Battleaxes and Formidable Aunties: The Daughter, the Sister and the Aunt: Sitt al-Mulk." In *Women and the Fatimids in the World of Islam*, 117–27. Edinburgh University Press, 2006.

"The Lady of Cairo." In *The Forgotten Queens of Islam*, edited by Fatima Mernissi and translated by Mary Jo Lakeland, 159–78. University of Minnesota Press, 1993.

Lev, Yaacov. "The Fātimid Princess Sitt Al-Mulk." *Journal of Semitic Studies* 32, no. 2 (1987): 319–28. https://doi.org/10.1093/jss/XXXII.2.319.

Walker, Paul E. "The Fatimid Caliph al-Aziz and His Daughter Sitt al-Mulk: A Case of Delayed but Eventual Succession to Rule by a Woman." *Journal of Persianate Studies* 4, no. 1 (2011): 30–44. https://doi.org/10.1163/187471611X568276.

———. "Social Elites at the Fatimid Court." In *Court Cultures in the Muslim World: Seventh to Nineteenth Centuries*, edited by Albrecht Fuess and Jan-Peter Hartung, 113–14. Routledge, 2011.

Elizabeth I

Borman, Tracy. *Elizabeth's Women: Friends, Rivals, and Foes Who Shaped the Virgin Queen.* Bantam, 2009.

———. "Robert Dudley: Queen Elizabeth I's Great Love." *History Extra*, January 8, 2016. https://www.historyextra.com/period/elizabethan/robert-dudley-queen-elizabeth-is-great-love/.

Marchant, Kat, host. "Dr Kat and The Virgin Queen." June 21, 2019. YouTube. https://www.youtube.com/watch?v=15_HXkkoaV8.

Neale, J. E. *Queen Elizabeth.* Penguin, 1971.

The Royal Family. "Elizabeth I (r. 1558–1603)." www.royal.uk/elizabeth-i.

Christina of Sweden

Brooklyn Museum. "Christina of Sweden." www.brooklynmuseum.org/eascfa/dinner_party/heritage_floor/christina_of_sweden.

"Christina of Sweden." In *Cyclopaedia of Female Biography: Consisting of Sketches of All Women Who Have Been Distinguished by Great Talents, Strength of Character, Piety, Benevolence, or Moral Virtue of Any Kind*, edited by Henry Gardiner Adams, 184–86. Routledge, 1869.

Compte, Deborah. "Two Portraits of a Queen: Calderón and the Enigmatic Christina of Sweden." *Hispanic Journal* 27, no. 1 (2006): 47–62. JSTOR. http://www.jstor.org/stable/44284801.

Gold, Claudia. "Christina Queen of Sweden." In *Queen, Empress, Concubine: Fifty Women Rulers from the Queen of Sheba to Catherine the Great*, 158–63. Quercus, 2008.

Schoenberg, Thomas J., and Lawrence J. Trudeau. "Christina of Sweden 1626–1689." In *Literature Criticism from 1400 to 1800*, vol. 124, 1–66. Thomson Gale, 2006.

Weibull, Curt. *Christina of Sweden.* Bonnier, 1966.

Zeb-un-Nissa

Dutta, Boni. "A Sufi Poetess of the Mughal Period: Zeb-un-Nisa." *International Journal of Emerging Technologies and Innovative Research (JETIR)* 7, no. 4 (2020): 12–13. https://www.jetir.org/view?paper=JETIR2004003.

Gupta, Subhadra Sen. *Mahal: Power and Pageantry in the Mughal Harem.* Hachette India, 2019.

Lal, Magan, and Jessie Duncan Westbrook. *The Diwan of Zeb-un-Nissa: The First Fifty Ghazals.* E. P. Dutton, 1913.

Mukherjee, Soma. "Learned Mughal Women of Aurangzeb's Times." In *Royal Mughal Ladies and Their Contribution*, 178–88. Gyan, 2001.

Sharma, Sunil. "Forbidden Love, Persianate Style: Re-Reading Tales of Iranian Poets and Mughal Patrons." *Iranian Studies* 42, no. 5 (2009): 765–79. https://doi.org/10.1080/00210860903306044.

Mkabayi kaJama

Eldredge, Elizabeth A. "Royal Women: Authority and Subservience." In *The Creation of the Zulu Kingdom, 1815–1828: War, Shaka, and the Consolidation of Power*, 172–204. Cambridge University Press, 2014.

Hanretta, Sean. "Women, Marginality, and the Zulu State: Women's Institutions and Power in the Early Nineteenth Century." *The Journal of African History* 39, no. 3 (1998): 389–415. JSTOR. https://www.jstor.org/stable/183360.

Masuku, Norma. "The Depiction of Mkabayi: A Review of Her Praise Poem." *South African Journal of African Languages* 29, no. 2 (2009): 121–30. https://doi.org/10.1080/025 72117.2009.10587323.

Nzimande, Makhosazana Keith. "Queen Mother Mkabayi kaJama Zulu: South Africa." In *African and European Readers of the Bible in Dialogue: In Quest of a Shared Meaning*, edited by Gerald West and Hans de Wit, 239–41. Brill, 2009.

Turner, Noleen S. "Comparison of the Izibongo of the Zulu Royal Women, Mnkabayi and Nandi." *South African Journal of African Languages* 8, no. 1 (1988): 28–33. https://doi.org/10.1080/02572117.1988.10586747.

Weir, Jennifer. "'I Shall Need to Use Her to Rule': The Power of 'Royal' Zulu Women in Pre-Colonial Zululand." *South African Historical Journal* 43, no. 1 (2000): 3–23. https://doi.org/10.1080/02582470008671905.

Dame Nita Barrow

Blackman, Woodie. *Dame Nita: Caribbean Woman, World Citizen.* Ian Randle, 1995.

———. "Obituary: Dame Nita Barrow." *The Independent*, December 22, 1995. www.independent.co.uk/news/people/obituary-dame-nita-barrow-1526933.html.

"Dame Ruth Nita Barrow, Ex-Barbados Governor General, 79." *The New York Times*, December 22, 1995. https://www.nytimes.com/1995/12/22/world/dame-ruth-nita-barrow-ex-barbados-governor-general-79.html.

Global Fund for Women. "Nita Barrow." https://www.globalfundforwomen.org/who-we-are/vision-mission/nita-barrow/.

"Shame on You, Mara for 'Childless' Remark!" *Barbados Today*, March 25, 2017. web.archive.org/web/20170325143430/http://www.barbadostoday.bb/2017/03/25/shame-on-you-mara-for-childless-remark/. "Memory of the World Register: Nita Barrow Collection." https://www.unesco.org/new/fileadmin/MULTIMEDIA/HQ/CI/CI/pdf/mow/nomination_forms/barbados_nita_barrow_collection.pdf.

UNESCO. "Memory of the World Register: Nita Barrow Collection." https://www.unesco.org/new/fileadmin/MULTIMEDIA/HQ/CI/CI/pdf/mow/nomination_forms/barbados_nita_barrow_collection.pdf.

Chapter 9: Embracing Individuality and Each Person's Unique Path

Ma Shouzhen

Blanchard, Lara C. W. "Imagining Du Liniang in *The Peony Pavilion*: Female Painters, Self-Portraiture, and Paintings of Beautiful Women in Late Ming China." In *Women, Gender and Art in Asia, c. 1500–1900*, edited by Melia Belli Bose, 125–46. Routledge, 2016.

Laing, Ellen Johnston. "Ma Shouzhen." In *Biographical Dictionary of Chinese Women, Volume II: Tang Through Ming, 618–1644*, edited by Lily Xiao Hong Lee and Sue Wiles. Taylor & Francis, 2014.

Merlin, Monica. "Life of a Chinese Courtesan: Ma Shouzhen (1548–1604)." *Aziatische Kunst* 38, no. 1 (2008): 16–22.

———. "The Nanjing Courtesan Ma Shouzhen (1548–1604): Gender, Space and Painting in the Late Ming Pleasure Quarter." *Gender & History* 23, no. 3 (2011): 630–652. https://doi.org/10.1111/j.1468-0424.2011.01660.x.

Zhao, Mi. "Ma Xianglan and Wang Zhideng Onstage and Offstage: Rethinking the Romance of a Courtesan Theatre in Ming-Qing China." *Asian Theatre Journal* 34, no. 1 (2017): 122–51. JSTOR. https://www.jstor.org/stable/44630741.

Jeanne Mance

Carpenter, Roger M. "Beaver Wars." In *The Encyclopedia of North American Indian Wars, 1607–1890: A Political, Social, and Military History*, edited by Spencer C. Tucker, 53–54. ABC-CLIO, 2011.

Daveluy, Marie-Claire. "Mance, Jeanne." In *Dictionary of Canadian Biography*, vol. 1. University of Toronto/Université Laval, 2017. https://www.biographi.ca/en/bio/mance_jeanne_1E.html.

Deslandres, Dominique. "In the Shadow of the Cloister: Representations of Female Holiness in New France." In *Colonial Saints: Discovering the Holy in the Americas, 1500–1800*, edited by Allan Greer and Jodi Bilinkoff, 129–52. Routledge, 2003.

Jaenen, C. J. "Le Ber, Jeanne." In *Dictionary of Canadian Biography*, vol. 2. University of Toronto/Université Laval, 1982. https://www.biographi.ca/en/bio/le_ber_jeanne_2E.html.

Kyle, Robert A., and Marc A. Shampo. "Jeanne Mance: Founder of Hôtel-Dieu of Montreal." *Mayo Clinic Proceedings* 63, no. 2 (1988): 212. doi:10.1016/s0025-6196(12)64962-3

Musée Pointe-à-Callière. "Jeanne Mance, Co-Founder of Montréal." https://pacmusee.qc.ca/en/stories-of-montreal/article/jeanne-mance-co-founder-of-montreal/.

Hester Lucy Stanhope

Barnhouse, Lucy, host. Footnoting History. "Desert Queens? Women at the Edges of Empire from Hester Stanhope to Gertrude Bell." June 4, 2016. Podcast. https://podtail.com/en/podcast/footnoting-history/desert-queens-women-at-the-edges-of-empire-fr/.

Haslip, Joan. *Lady Hester Stanhope: The Unconventional Life of the "Queen of the Desert."* Sutton, 2006.

Paston, George. "Lady Hester Stanhope." In *Little Memoirs of the Nineteenth Century*, 217–76. Grant Richards, 1902.

Strachey, Lytton. "Lady Hester Stanhope." In *Biographical Essays*, 211–18. Harcourt Brace Jovanovich, 1969.

Dr. Margaret Chung

Harris, Gloria G., and Hannah S. Cohen. "Margaret 'Mom' Chung: First Chinese American Physician in California." In *Women Trailblazers of California*, 104–7. The History Press, 2012.

Rasmussen, Cecilia. "Chinese American Was 'Mom' to 1,000 Servicemen." *Los Angeles Times*, June 24, 2001. https://www.latimes.com/archives/la-xpm-2001-jun-24-me-14223-story.html.

Wu, Judy Tzu-Chun. *Doctor Mom Chung of the Fair-Haired Bastards: The Life of a Wartime Celebrity*. University of California Press, 2005.

Greta Garbo

Bainbridge, John. *Garbo*. Doubleday, 1955.

Barnes, Bart. "Greta Garbo Dies at Age 84." *The Washington Post*, April 16, 1990. https://www.washingtonpost.com/archive/politics/1990/04/16/greta-garbo-dies-at-age-84/2392db2c-43ad-4a5f-b801-1daa478e8d79/.

Bianco, Marcie, and Merryn Johns. "When the Oscars Began, It Was the Women Who Had All the Power." *Vanity Fair*, February 10, 2016. https://www.vanityfair.com/hollywood/2016/02/oscar-history-gender.

Willie Mae Thornton

Denise, Lynnée. *Why Willie Mae Thornton Matters*. University of Texas Press, 2023.

Gaar, Gillian G. "Roots." In *She's a Rebel: The History of Women in Rock & Roll*, 1–4. Seal Press, 1992.

Shadwick, Keith. "Big Mama Thornton." In *The Encyclopedia of Jazz & Blues*, 653. Quintet, 2001.

Shapiro, Ari, and Maureen Mahon. "How Bessie Smith Influenced a Century of Popular Music." *NPR*, August 5, 2019. https://www.npr.org/transcripts/747738120.

Thornton, Willie Mae, and Chris Strachwitz. "Big Mama Thornton Interview." Arhoolie Foundation. https://arhoolie.org/big-mama-thornton-interview/.

Colette Magny

Barron, Hannah, and Vincent Decque. "Colette Magny (1926–1997), Colère Géante." *France Culture*, March 7, 2020. https://www.franceculture.fr/emissions/une-vie-une-oeuvre/colette-magny-colere-geante-1926-1997.

Houzé, Benoît. "Colette Magny (1926–1997): A Pop Avant-Gardist." In *An Anthology of French and Francophone Singers from A to Z*, edited by Michaël Abecassis and Marcelline Block, 431–34. Cambridge Scholars, 2018.

Mazerolle, Valérie. "Quand la Chanson Se Fait Violence: Analyse Sociosémiotique du Répertoire de Colette Magny (1967–1972)." In *La Voix & le Geste: Une Approche Culturelle de la Violence Socio-politique*, edited by Mathias Bernard, Philippe Bourdin, and Jean-Claude Caron, 339–58. Presses Universitaires Blaise Pascal, 2005.

Perrone, Pierre. "Obituary: Colette Magny." *The Independent*, June 25, 1997. https://www.independent.co.uk/news/people/obituary-colette-magny-1257858.html.

Florence King

Ennis, Dawn. "Remembering Florence King, Conservative Lesbian Feminist." *The Advocate*, January 11, 2016. https://www.advocate.com/women/2016/1/11/remembering-florence-king-conservative-lesbian-feminist.

Fox, Margalit. "Florence King, Writer Who Wielded an Acerbic Wit, Dies at 80." *The New York Times*, January 9, 2016. https://www.nytimes.com/2016/01/10/arts/florence-king-writer-who-wielded-an-acerbic-wit-dies-at-80.html.

King, Florence. *Confessions of a Failed Southern Lady*. St. Martin's Press, 1985.

———. "Staunch Spinsters Give Women a Good Name." *Los Angeles Times*, August 10, 1986. https://www.latimes.com/archives/la-xpm-1986-08-10-op-2516-story.html.

Seidel, Matt. "Everybody Stinks: The Life & Work of Florence King." *The Millions*, April 27, 2016. https://themillions.com/2016/04/everybody-stinks-life-work-failed-southern-lady.html.

Chapter 10: Protectors of People, Culture, and Language

Manuela Cañizares

Cevallos, Pedro Fermín. "Capítulo II: Conspiración del 2 de Agosto." In *Resumen de la Historia del Ecuador Desde su Orijen Hasta 1845*, vol. 3. Cervantes Virtual, n.d. https://www.cervantesvirtual.com/obra-visor/pedro-fermin-cevallos--0/html/fffd854e-82b1-11df-acc7-002185ce6064_11.html#I_15_.

Cherpak, Evelyn. "The Participation of Women in the Independence Movement in Gran Colombia, 1780–1830." In *Latin American Women: Historical Perspectives*, edited by Asunción Lavrin, 220. Greenwood Press, 1978.

"First Cry of Independence." Posted August 6, 2014, by the Consulado del Ecuador en Caracas. YouTube. https://www.youtube.com/watch?v=SVuBmBH7kTg.

Polanco, Manuel de Guzmán. *Manuela Cañizares: La heroína de la independencia del Ecuador*. La Comisión Nacional Permanente de Conmemoraciones Cívicas, 2006.

———. "Manuela Cañizares y Álvarez." In *Diccionario Biográfico Español*. Real Academia de la Historia. https://dbe.rah.es/biografias/87017/manuela-canizares-y-alvarez.

Salazar, Sonia, and Alexandra Sevilla. "Las Mujeres y su Participación Activa en la Revolución de Quito 1809-1812." Revista de la Asociación de Funcionarios y Empleados del Servicio Exterior del Ecuador. https://www.afese.com/img/revistas/revista51/mujeresrevo.pdf.

Torrente, Mariano. *Historia de la Revolución Hispano-americana*. Leon Amarita, 1829.

Lozen

Bannan, Helen M. "Lozen." In *Native American Women: A Biographical Dictionary*, edited by Gretchen M. Bataille and Laurie Lisa, 190–91. Routledge, 2001.

Leach, Mike, and Buddy Levy. "Woman Warrior: Lozen." In *Geronimo: Leadership Strategies of an American Warrior*, 78–81. Gallery Books, 2014.

Rangel, Valerie. "The Story of Lozen: Apache Woman Warrior, Seer, Healer, Midwife, and Sister to Chihenne Apache Chief Victorio." New Mexico History, July 21, 2015. https://www.newmexicohistory.org/2015/07/21/the-story-of-lozen/.

Encarnación Pinedo

"Encarnación Pinedo." Santa Clara University Digital Collections. https://content.scu.edu/digital/collection/pinedo.

Pinedo, Encarnación. *Encarnación's Kitchen: Mexican Recipes from Nineteenth-Century California*, edited by Dan Strehl. University of California Press, 2003.

Ruiz, Vicki L. "Pinedo, Encarnación." In *Latinas in the United States: A Historical Encyclopedia*, edited by Vicki L. Ruiz and Virginia Sánchez-Korrol, 576–77. Indiana University Press, 2006.

Strehl, Dan. "Pinedo, Encarnación." In *The Oxford Encyclopedia of Food and Drink in America*, edited by Andrew F. Smith, 2nd ed., vol. 1, 7–8. Oxford University Press, 2012.

Angelina Weld Grimké

Grimké, Angelina Weld. *Rachel*. The Cornhill Company, 1920.

———. *Selected Works of Angelina Weld Grimké*, edited by Carolivia Herron. Oxford University Press, 1991.

Hull, Gloria T. "Angelina Weld Grimké (1880–1958)." In *Color, Sex & Poetry: Three Women Writers of the Harlem Renaissance*, 106–52. Indiana University Press, 1987.

Shockley, Ann Allen. "Angelina Weld Grimké (1880–1958)." In *Afro-American Women Writers, 1746–1933: An Anthology and Critical Guide*, 373–79. New American Library, 1989.

Betsie ten Boom and Corrie ten Boom

Ten Boom, Corrie, and Carole C. Carlson. *In My Father's House: The Years Before "The Hiding Place."* Fleming H. Revell Company, 1976.

Ten Boom, Corrie, Elizabeth Sherrill, and John Sherrill. *The Hiding Place.* Guideposts, 1971.

"The History of the Museum." Corrie ten Boom Museum. https://www.corrietenboom.com/en/information/the-history-of-the-museum.

May Ziadeh

Booth, Marilyn. "Biography and Feminist Rhetoric in Early Twentieth-Century Egypt: Mayy Ziyada's Studies of Three Women's Lives." *Journal of Women's History* 3, no. 1 (1991): 38–64. https://doi.org/10.1353/jowh.2010.0118.

Boustani, Carmen. "May Ziadé: Vie et Écriture." *Les Cahiers du GRIF* 43–44 (1990): 163–69. Persée. https://www.persee.fr/doc/grif_0770-6081_1990_num_43_1_1836.

Ghorayeb, Rose. "May Ziadeh (1886–1941)." *Signs* 5, no. 2 (1979): 375–82. JSTOR. http://www.jstor.org/stable/3173578.

"May Ziade: The Life of an Arab Feminist Writer." *Al Jazeera*, March 21, 2018. https://www.aljazeera.com/programmes/aljazeeraworld/2018/03/ziade-life-arab-feminist-writer-180318140908795.html.

Naccach, Nessrine. "Break and Enter: May Ziadé and Jocelyne Saab: Words and Images for the Use of the 'Dés-orientale'." *Trayectorias Humanas Trascontinentales* 6 (2019). http://dx.doi.org/10.25965/trahs.1833.

Rachad, A. "May Ziadé." *Les Nouvelles Littéraires* 12, no. 522 (1934): 8. Gallica. https://gallica.bnf.fr/ark:/12148/bpt6k6452196d/f8.item.r=%22may%20ziade%22.zoom.

Vivian G. Harsh

Burt, Laura. "Vivian Harsh, Adult Education, and the Library's Role as Community Center." *Libraries and the Cultural Record* 44, no. 2 (2009): 234–55. https://doi.org/10.1353/lac.0.0071.

Chicago Public Library. "Vivian G. Harsh: Librarian of the Chicago Black Renaissance." April 18, 2016. https://www.chipublib.org/blogs/post/vivian-g-harsh-librarian-of-the-chicago-black-renaissance/.

———. "Vivian G. Harsh Research Collection of Afro-American History and Literature." https://www.chipublib.org/vivian-g-harsh-research-collection/.

Grossman, Ron. "Flashback: A Heroine to History: Vivian Harsh, Chicago's First Black Librarian, Preserved Black History, Literature with Massive Collection." *Chicago Tribune*, January 31, 2020. https://www.chicagotribune.com/2020/01/31/flashback-a-heroine-to-history-vivian-harsh-chicagos-first-black-librarian-preserved-black-history-literature-with-massive-collection/.

Gladys Tantaquidgeon

Fawcett, Melissa Jayne. *Medicine Trail: The Life and Lessons of Gladys Tantaquidgeon*. University of Arizona Press, 2000.

"Gladys Tantaquidgeon." Connecticut Women's Hall of Fame. www.cwhf.org/inductees/gladys-tantaquidgeon.

"Gladys Tantaquidgeon." Mohegan Tribe Official Website. www.mohegan.nsn.us/explore/heritage/memoriam/medicine-woman-gladys-tantaquidgeon-memorial.

"Gladys Tantaquidgeon, 106, Mohegans' Medicine Woman." *The New York Times*, November 2, 2005. https://www.nytimes.com/2005/11/02/us/gladys-tantaquidgeon-106-mohegans-medicine-woman.html.

Turner, Erin H. "Gladys Tantaquidgeon." In *Wise Women: From Pocahontas to Sarah Winnemucca, Remarkable Stories of Native American Trailblazers*, 93–103. TwoDot, 2009.

Mridula Sarabhai

Basu, Aparna. "A Nationalist Feminist: Mridula Sarabhai (1911–1974)." *Indian Journal of Gender Studies* 2, no. 1 (1995): 1–24. https://doi.org/10.1177/097152159500200101.

———. "Sarabhai, Mridula." In *The Oxford Encyclopedia of Women in World History*, vol. 1, edited by Bonnie G. Smith, 637. Oxford University Press, 2008.

Chakravarti, Uma. "Archiving Disquiet: Feminist Praxis and the Nation-State." In *Human Rights and Peace: Ideas, Laws, Institutions and Movements*, edited by Ujjwal Kumar Singh, 55–62. SAGE Publications, 2009.

Minault, Gail. "Review of 'Mridula Sarabhai: Rebel with a Cause,' by Aparna Basu." *The American Historical Review* 102, no. 4 (1997): 1216. https://doi.org/10.2307/2170751.

———. "Review of 'Borders and Boundaries: Women in India's Partition,' by Ritu Menon and Kamla Bhasin." *The Journal of Asian Studies*, 58, no. 3 (1999): 871–72. https://doi.org/10.2307/2659179.

Enjoy *Unwed & Unbothered* as an audiobook, wherever audiobooks are sold.